EFFECTIVE COLLEGE MANAGEMENT

Effective College Management

THE OUTCOME APPROACH

Bruce W. Tuckman and F. Craig Johnson

PRAEGER

New York
Westport, Connecticut
London

Library of Congress Cataloging-in-Publication Data

Tuckman, Bruce W., 1938-
  Effective college management.

  Includes bibliographical references.
  1. Universities and colleges—United States—
Administration.   I. Johnson, F. Craig.   II. Title.
LB2341.T79 1987   378.73   87–2573
ISBN 0–275–92730-X (alk. paper)

Library of Congress Catalog Card Number: 87–2573
ISBN: 0–275–92730-X
First published in 1987

Praeger Publishers, One Madison Avenue, New York, NY 10010
A division of Greenwood Press, Inc.

Printed in the United States of America

The paper used in this book complies with the Permanent
Paper Standard issued by the National Information Standards
Organization (Z39.48–1984).

10 9 8 7 6 5 4 3 2 1

To Erb Fontenot, colleague and friend

Contents

Preface

This book has been written because administrators, like ourselves, in colleges and universities are faced with mounting financial pressures and increased requirements for accountability. To meet these pressures and requirements, we must make our budgets go further and get more productivity from our faculty members.

This book is designed to show other administrators of higher education institutions how to use information management, planning, and resource allocation strategies to increase faculty productivity and make more rational decisions. The techniques we describe focus on specific outcomes to be achieved and management techniques to achieve them. What is new about the overall strategy offered in this book is its comprehensiveness and its applicability. It covers many techniques for managing any and all desired outcomes, and its approach has been tried on the firing line by working administrators, ourselves. It is more than just the ideas of theoreticians or the findings of researchers.

We have written about outcome management for both working administrators and those training to fill that role, from university and college presidents and vice presidents, through deans and division directors, to department heads and program leaders. We have presented detailed procedures to help such administrators manage (or prepare to manage) the academic organization under their immediate jurisdiction. We have provided the administrator or manager with an operational model called outcome management, instructions for implementing that model including goal setting, measuring, managing information, planning, and allocating resources, as well as analyses to show how these instructions are to be applied and interrelated, and the results of the process.

All of this "user-friendly" information is set in a practical and understandable context. Since the distinction between academic and practical or between theoretical and applied is quite fuzzy in the area of higher education administration (let's face it, all college administrators are both practitioners and academics), we have taken pains to blend the practical and theoretical, the concrete and abstract, into what might be called a "working theory." We have gone beyond ideas into practice. And we have done this mainly on the basis of the case study which represents the fabric into which the ideas of the book are woven.

The case study, based on a large college of education that we administrated over a two-year period, illustrates in practical terms the application of the outcome management model. Within the college, we set goals to be attained, established measures of their attainment as the basis for a management information system, planned the way to go about meeting the goals, and allocated the resources at our disposal as a function of the productivity of efforts to reach those goals. While the ideas and procedures we present are clearly not limited to just the single case situation within which they were developed, the case study does provide a vehicle for making our management theory into something more than just a thought. A community college president who read an early draft of this work commented that he found the outcome management model to be not only "impersonal, data-oriented, fair, and successful," but a "practical guide to distributing and managing resources." This suggests that we have hit our mark.

The first two chapters of the book focus on the model itself—why and under what conditions it was developed, what its strengths and limitations are, what principles it is based on, exactly what it looks like, and how it is to be applied. The next two chapters deal with the specification and measurement of goal attainment in terms of productivity in instruction, research, and service. This is the management information system and it is described in detail, including specifics about data collection.

The next two chapters are devoted to the planning process, the mechanism by which strategies for attaining goals can be decided upon and operationalized. Again, highly specific proposals are offered along with some likely outcomes based on actual practice. Then come two chapters about decision making based on the application of the outcome management model. The first of these chapters is concerned with the allocation of resources, particularly unfilled positions, to programs, while the second describes procedures for the distribution of dollars to individual faculty members. Both use the outcome-oriented approach of the model and both are detailed and operational in their descriptions and instructions. The final chapter outlines both the successes and failures of outcome management as a strategy for organizational management within the context of the college environment. Again, the emphasis is on practicality and results.

This book represents to us a sharing of ideas and experiences with all other college and university administrators who want to make a difference and who regard excellence as the goal in spite of the continuing shrinkage of available resources and the limitations in flexibility regarding personnel. We believe that outcome management is the route to goal attainment and that goal attainment is the reason behind being an administrator. We built a system for investing our resources in performance and we had the chance to try it out. We would like to offer you that same chance.

1

Background of the Book

We are in a period of intense self-examination and change in the field of organizational management. The precipitating factor for this state of flux is unquestionably economic, in particular, the success of corporations from other nations, principally Japan, relative to those in the United States. We have arrived at the point where Yankee ingenuity is not enough to keep our country at the top of world markets.

It appeared that the manner in which organizations were being managed was an important factor in the current productivity equation, and we first looked at Japanese corporations to try to understand better what effective management practices might be. The result was the emergence of so-called theory Z, a complex concept involving significant elements of participation by workers in managerial decisions (Ouchi, 1981).

But Japan is culturally different from the United States and Japanese techniques did not transfer well to our settings, so attention shifted from successful Japanese companies to successful American companies. The result was a book that has become the focus of interest in organizational management circles, *In Search of Excellence* (Peters & Waterman, 1982). This book raised two major points of emphasis. The first was on the importance of outcomes and their attainment. It was excellence as measured by sustained corporate growth that was to be pursued. In order to qualify as a "best run" company, you had to attain your goals and, in the corporate business world, those goals are ultimately financial ones. No management technique is worth studying if it does not somehow result in increased profitability.

The second point was that organizational management principles should be anchored primarily at three levels, none of which are the managers themselves. The three levels are the employees, the customers, and the product. The idea is to link means and ends. If the end is a better product, then the means must be quality control. If the end is a more satisfied customer, then the means must be customer service. If the end is a more productive employee, then the means must be maximizing employee opportunities and rewards for productivity.

It is difficult to translate these principles from the corporate business setting to that of the schools, colleges, and universities. Part of the problem is the difficulty inherent in defining excellence in the educational setting. What is the educational counterpart of profits? If it is student learning, then what is it the learning of, and how can that learning be measured? It is far easier for companies to determine whether they are making money than for schools to determine whether students are learning. The result has been for schools to focus on only one or two learning outcomes, and this focus has the potential for undesirable side effects.

A MANAGEMENT MODEL FOR EDUCATION

This book evolves, describes, and demonstrates the usefulness of a management model for colleges and universities that focuses on the attainment of excellence as an end product. Excellence is defined as the direct result of organization member behaviors, that is, faculty, in order to place the responsibility for the outcomes on the behavior of the managers, that is, administrators, since they are directly in a position to influence faculty members' behavior.

The decision to focus on faculty members' behavior is based on the inherent difficulty in getting comparative data on student behavior or in linking student outcomes directly to the behavior of faculty. Unlike companies in the business world, which have a reasonably constant inflow of information on profits, the so-called bottom line, universities have no comparable measure of their outcomes or effects. Since the approach we have chosen to use focuses on desirable outcomes and how they can be maximized at minimal cost, it is necessary that there be outcomes that can be specified and measured and that performance on these outcomes be ones that can be directly affected by administrative decisions. These requirements are more readily met at the faculty level than at the student level. The same requirements would apply to the use of an outcome management model in any type of institution, but since it is only in the business world where ultimate outcomes can be measured in profit and loss, dollars-and-cents terms, all other types of institutions would find it necessary to deal with outcomes at the level of employees rather than of clients.

The model that we propose is called outcome management; it represents a method of attempting to maximize organizational outcomes by maximizing individual contributions. First, it uses performance as its outcome measure, and second, it bases the allocation of resources on the quantity and quality of performance. The more or better an academic unit or individual faculty member performs, the more the performer gains in terms of resources to be allocated. Third, it uses information or data as a basis for evaluating performance levels and detecting performance improvement. By comparing measurable outcomes at two points in time, changes in performance can be seen. Fourth, it uses goals as the basis for deciding what performances are desirable, that is, that will help the organization. Some goals are broader and more general and may apply across the organization while others may be more specific to individual units. Fifth, it employs planning as the means by which actions are decided upon relative to the purposes of goal attainment and outcome maximization. And sixth, it is dynamic and self-correcting in that goals (i.e., desired outcomes), plans (i.e., steps to achieve goals), measures (i.e., information used to detect progress toward goal attainment), and rewards (i.e., resources received for performance) can and will all be adjusted in order to increase the likelihood of attaining organizational goals.

Why have we selected this particular model and why do we think it will work? Consider the following fable. A weekend fisherman looked over the side of his boat and saw a snake with a frog in its mouth. Feeling sorry for the frog, he reached down, gently removed the frog from the snake's mouth, and let the frog go free. But now he felt sorry for the hungry snake. Having no food, he took out a flask of bourbon and poured a few drops into the snake's mouth. The snake swam away happy, the frog was happy, and the man was happy for having performed such good deeds. He thought all was well until a few minutes passed and he heard something knock against the side of his boat and looked down. With stunned disbelief, the fisherman saw the snake was back—with two frogs!

The fable leads to two conclusions. The first is that you get more of the behavior you reward (rather than more of the behavior you desire, choose, value, or hope to get). Both individuals and organizations do more of what pays off. Second, if we reward the wrong behaviors and ignore or punish the right ones, we will get more of the wrong ones and less of the right ones. We in higher education often talk about performance as desirable but tend instead to reward all units and individuals the same or on the basis of other factors, such as influence or political power, rather than actual, observable performance.

On a theoretical level, the model is consistent with the theory of organizations proposed by March and Simon (1958). March and Simon have proposed that effective management requires that organization members be induced to make maximal contributions toward the organization meeting its goals. The outcome management model can be used simultaneously to further any goals selected by the organization so that individual rewards would be apportioned according to individual performance on these goals.

It is important, however, that the proposed model is not specific in terms of either goals or means. Each user of the model, either individually or organizationally, may choose whatever goals he or she prefers and then propose whatever means or methods seem most likely to lead to attainment of those goals. In other words, the model is a mechanism for goal attainment, irrespective of either the specific goals themselves or the methods for reaching the goals. However, when the model is actually used as part of a management system, the goals must be specified and concretized.

CONTEXT FOR THE CASE STUDY

In this book we do more than describe the model as a prospective or potential tool for college administrators; we also show how it actually was used and with what results. We accomplish this second purpose through the vehicle of a case study of a single college, in this instance a college of education, within which the model was evolved and put to use. The college we use is a large and complex one with seven departments that collectively contain 22 programs and 145 faculty. We draw many illustrations from this college because it makes our points clearer and easier to follow.

Within the illustrative case, the model described in this book was not preconceived, that is, generated in total in advance of its use, and it was not put to use in pure form. The organization in which it was used was not merely a subject for study but an ongoing organization with real needs and real problems. In the course of trying to meet those needs and solve those problems, we evolved and implemented the model as described in this book. Hence, the book represents a cast study of one organization from a retrospective point of view.

The development and application of the outcome management model in the specific case of a college of education represents an appropriate test in a number of respects. Colleges of education have been particularly vulnerable to charges of low quality and excess staffing and are under particular pressure to demonstrate sound management. Colleges of education, however, have long had company with respect to budget cuts. The model will be useful in any academic unit faced with the need to control costs and increase productivity.

OUTCOMES TO BE ATTAINED

Since outcome management requires that there be a set of organizational goals or desired outcomes for which plans of attainment will be made and which form the basis for the allocation of resources, the case study required that such goals be specified. These goals would then be used to guide the college of education (which was the subject of the case study) in carrying out each of the succeeding steps in the model. Three general goals, described below, were set by the administration after a careful and detailed analysis of the state of the college, and were presented to the faculty of the college in order both to inform them and gain their concurrence. Subsequent stages of the model would then focus on the translation of these general goals into more specific program goals by each program's faculty and the development of plans by faculty members to attain these goals. In conceptual terms, these goals were labeled responsiveness, recognition, and efficiency.

Responsiveness refers to the extent to which the organization responds to needs that are found to exist in either the operation of the organization itself or in the context in which the organization exists. In the case of a college of education, these needs are generated by the public education sector at all levels. Behavior that is intended to be responsive is referred to as *service*, and the magnitude or degree to which such service is manifested is labeled *service productivity*. In order to sustain its own functions as well as to serve public need, higher education organizations need to produce service.

Recognition refers to the extent to which the organization has raised itself to a level of significant awareness within its own professional circles. Recognition can be an important factor in efforts to recruit both students and faculty. Behavior that is intended to gain recognition is *research*, and the degree to which such research is done is *research productivity*. The basic research unit may be either the published research article or the research contract or grant.

Efficiency refers to the extent to which the organization can fulfill its responsibilities within its financial means. The formal responsibilities of a college are *instructional* and include teaching classes and advising graduate students. The degree of performance in the area of instruction for a given amount of cost is termed *instructional productivity*.

Thus, we have arrived at the commonly accepted trinity of academe—instruction, research, and service—as the three outcomes to be managed within the outcome management model. Each is chosen as an element of the attainment of excellence by a college or other academic unit. Each is evaluated solely in terms of productivity, that is, how much of it occurs.

Naming instruction, research, and service as organizational goals is quite traditional, at least on paper, but quite unconventional in practice. First, such outcomes are rarely employed in the evaluation of programs; their presumed use is typically restricted to individual faculty members. Second, even in the evaluation of individual faculty members, such goals are seldom the basis for criteria in annual ratings and discretionary raise decisions. Instead, the use of instruction, research, and service evaluations is restricted to decisions of tenure and promotion. Third, while all three may be named as goals, often only research is considered because it appears to be the only one that can be counted. In fact, all three can be quantified, and should be, because it is grossly unfair to consider only one as a measure of quantity yet attempt to evaluate the other two in terms of quality. Fourth, in the final analysis, performances in each of three areas are rarely viewed in terms of productivity, perhaps because productivity can be quantified and hence direct comparisons between faculty members can be made. Such comparisons are often considered threatening.

Have we oversimplified the complexities of the goals of higher education institutions? From the organization's point of view, the quality of instruction is of little importance if relatively little takes place or if most is assigned to graduate students. The faculty member who "toils in the trenches," year after year, teaching multitudes of students in introductory courses as his or her major activity, will receive much organizational credit in a system that measures, values, and rewards instructional productivity in quantitative terms. In the absence of quantitative instructional goals, instruction is essentially disregarded in the faculty performance equation since few have been able to agree, over the years, on what constitutes effective instruction and few are willing to accept student evaluations as measures of anything except "popularity."

In terms of research, our findings show that those who produce products in one form, such as journal articles, also produce products in all other forms, from books to professional papers to unpublished papers, while those who do not produce products in one form also do not produce products in the other forms. In simple terms, our colleges are staffed by researchers, that is, those who produce all forms of research, and nonresearchers, that is, those who produce no forms of research. If the organizational value of research is to enhance the organization's recognition and if all forms of research are interchangeable, it makes best sense to use as a measure of research productivity the form that has the potentially greatest readership, the journal article. Moreover, journal articles are reviewed and evaluated prior to acceptance for publication, which makes them a qualitative as well as a quantitative measure.

Finally, service gets even less lip service than instruction and even less recognition. Yet when one examines the assignment forms for faculty in the college under consideration, service accounts for an average of 15 percent of faculty time. Given an annual faculty payroll of $4 million, service is costing the organization more than half a million dollars. Surely the organization has a right to expect some productivity in return.

It would seem that our three goals are sufficiently complete and inclusive to cover all of the significant performance dimensions of the members of higher education organizations and will not seem to represent an oversimplifying of the academic role.

THE UNIT AND THE PURPOSE

In applying the outcome management model, it is necessary to determine the organizational unit or units that will be used for purposes of analysis, planning, and resource allocation. The goals that are set and plans made to meet those goals must have a locus and there must be some subset of people to whom resources can be allocated. There are four academic units available upon whose outcomes focus can be placed. These are (1) the individual faculty member, (2) the program, (3) the department, and (4) the college. The most appropriate unit would be one that has a reasonably high degree of homogeneity in terms of the backgrounds, interests, and goals of its participants so that goals may be shared among members of a unit.

In the case study, the program proved to be the most suitable unit. There were 22 programs in the college ranging in size from two to eight members with the majority at four to six members. Programs were originally constituted in the college on the base of discipline and areas of interest so that programs could be expected to be quite homogeneous in terms of the goals of both faculty and students. Therefore, the program was the unit of focus both in terms of the collection of performance data and the planning process. Also, resource allocation could be done on a program basis rather than on a department basis because of the programs' greater homogeneity.

Individual faculty also served as a unit of analysis in regard to academic assignments, annual evaluations, and the allocation of salary raises. The department and college were both too large and too heterogeneous to serve as units of analysis or decision making for purposes of applying the outcome management model. Despite the traditional use of the department as a unit for most university-wide analyses, it was impractical to use as a unit for planning and consensus building within the case of the college of education. In liberal arts colleges, however, the departments are typically more homogeneous and may be more useful as units of analysis.

The purpose of having a unit of analysis and decision making is to make it possible and meaningful for individual faculty members to work together to achieve common goals. The university is a highly idiopathic institution, that is, the members of the university organization, namely, faculty, work primarily to achieve individual goals. These individual goals do not always correspond to organizational goals. Faculty members sometimes use organizational resources such as space and secretarial services to carry out functions from which the university may not profit, such as their own private consulting work.

However, the extent to which an organization will thrive depends on the contributions its members make to it (March & Simon, 1958). The purpose of outcome management is to make the organization thrive, that is, to maximize organizational outcomes by managing to maximize individual organizational contributions. The level or unit of the organization to which these contributions can be made is the one that is most homogeneous, which, in the case study, was the program. In some academic areas, the department may be sufficiently small or homogeneous to serve as an appropriate unit of analysis. Classics or art history would be two such examples.

Is it reasonable to expect a highly idiopathic or individualistic institution like a university to function in a nomothetic or norm-sharing, common interest way? The answer is yes, if the degree of correspondence or overlap of individual goals and organizational goals is high. Theoretically, this is the case for universities. If individual faculty members are, in fact, evaluated, promoted, and rewarded for their instructional, research, and service productivity, and if programs acquire resources on the basis of their responsiveness, recognition, and efficiency, then individual contributions are likely to be maximized.

However, if individual goals are for protection, security, and independence to make more outside income and these individual goals do not contribute to the organizational goals of responsiveness, recognition, and efficiency, then individuals will not make organizational contributions and the organization will cease to exist in a functional sense.

The purpose of outcome management, which is the attainment of organizational excellence, therefore requires that individual faculty members endorse productivity goals, make plans to meet productivity goals, carry out these plans, and receive rewards both individually and organizationally.

The process of outcome management requires that productivity be measured at both the individual and organizational (in this case, program) levels, that organizational plans be formulated to increase productivity and that the results of this planned activity be measured, and that organizational resources be allocated according to these results.

PLAN OF THE BOOK

Our chapters focus on the various aspects of performance or productivity measurement as part of a management information system in order to show others exactly how to put these systems in place. These same chapters also deal with our growing ability to understand the various individual and organizational processes by looking at relationships among data collected to form the management information system. Beyond that we look at the planning process, some of its concrete manifestations, and some concrete approaches for facilitating it.

More specifically, we first describe both the theoretical basis for the model and the model itself and offer additional arguments in support of its use. Then we provide detailed descriptions of the specification and measurement of performance outcomes of both programs and individual faculty members in the areas of instruction and noninstruction, that is, research and service. This description is done within the case study so that we can use the concrete measures of performance that were incorporated into an actual management information system. The focus here is on the description and evaluation of performance.

In the next part of the book we focus directly on the planning process, again primarily within the context of the case study. Here, we describe how individuals and programs can identify the steps to be undertaken in order to attain goals. Specific planning techniques and procedures are described, all of which were used within the case study.

Next, we apply the outcome management model to administrative decision making and show how it can be used. Again, we rely primarily on demonstration, drawing from the case study. Two kinds of administrative decisions are examined and described, both of which can be facilitated by the proposed model. The first includes decisions about allocating resources, such as staff positions, to specific academic units; the second involves allocating discretionary raise money to individual faculty. Both are critical areas and both sets of analyses will be based on actual experiences.

Finally, we look at results. We try honestly to face up to the strengths and limitations of outcome management. For this, we again draw on the experience of the case study, but we also generalize from it to other academic situations.

CAN OUTCOME MANAGEMENT WORK?

Outcome management is both a belief and a tool. It is a belief that within the university setting, the organizational unit—be it a program, department, school, college, or division—must have goals and meet those goals if the university is to be a maximal contributor to society. To this end, individual faculty members must bring their goals into line with organizational goals, not only philosophically but operationally as well, in order for the organization to succeed in goal attainment.

Can outcome management work? Will it work? In order to answer these questions, we must first examine the operational rules that must be followed in carrying it out and the degree of overlap between these rules and the existing "rules" by which universities typically operate. We will proceed both theoretically and empirically in this effort. We will describe how the system should operate and how, in an actual instance, it did operate. Insofar as possible, we shall examine the immediate empirical results of each step relative to the context in which it occurred.

Outcome management is not intended as the end-all or be-all of higher education. It will not help an administrator to become a better communicator or listener or to become more skillful in relating to other people. There are many other dimensions of effective management beyond the making of goals and plans and the measurement of progress toward them. At best, outcome management may be seen as a necessary management tool but surely not a sufficient one, in and of itself.

By the same token, though, communicating and relating are not enough to keep organizations moving. Organizations, be they businesses or colleges, must have direction and accountability. We have chosen to focus on the aspects of direction and consequences primarily because of their seeming absence from the college conference room. But this emphasis on outcomes and their attainment is not meant to suggest that relating to faculty is not an important part of an administrator's job. Good management requires both a system and the personal skills to make it work. In this book, we have chosen to focus on the system or model for management.

What we offer here are ideas that have been tried. These ideas were shaped and honed on the forge of real-world administration. We were not observers nor were we researchers. Our motive was not to discover or uncover. We were accountable and we needed ideas to guide us. What is about to unfold before you are the ideas, how we translated those ideas into action, and the results of that action. You be the judge.

2

The Outcome Management Model

In this chapter we will provide a description of the principles behind the model and the model itself and then address some cogent questions about the model's potential use.

SOME PRINCIPLES OF INDIVIDUAL AND ORGANIZATIONAL BEHAVIOR

The outcome management model is based on a number of principles of human behavior that can be applied to the human performance situation. Taken together, these principles suggest the approach we have called outcome management. There is no one-to-one correspondence between the principles enumerated below and the steps in the model, but the principles do help provide a rationale for the model as a total entity.

The Principle of Individual Information Exposure

In social comparison theory, Festinger (1954) posits that people judge themselves and their own performances in comparison to the performances of others to determine how well or poorly they have done. Given an inherent motivation to evaluate one's own abilities, a person will inevitably use others as a point of reference, especially when physical reality checks are not available. The people one uses as the basis for such comparisons are often referred to as one's reference group.

As a corollary of social comparison theory, one can postulate that when information about oneself or one's own performance is exposed or made available to others, one will anticipate that others will use it for social comparison purposes and, therefore, one will be highly motivated to maximize that performance. In other words, we all want to put our best foot forward when someone else, especially members of our reference group, will view our work so that we can see ourselves as potentially comparing favorably with others.

It is remarkable in higher education how often each faculty member's work is shrouded by a veil of privacy from his or her immediate colleagues. It is well recognized that to be a "prophet in one's own land" is rare and that the further one gets from home, the more recognition one receives. Each professor is insulated against social comparison with his or her immediate peers by remaining unfamiliar with the productive work of others, in terms of either quality or quantity.

To invoke the principle of information exposure as a productivity motivator by way of the social comparison phenomenon, one need only make information about the performance of individuals or of programs publicly available in a readily understood format and through a readily accessible medium. Of course, one who would collect performance information and make it available must recognize that many faculty members will, when faced with the specter of social comparison, actively attempt to subvert the collection process or suppress the exposure process. In other words, the motivation of some, particularly those of low self-assessed performance, will manifest itself, not in an effort to perform better but to prevent someone else from exposing their performance to others. Hence, this principle represents a double-edged sword.

In the outcome management model, many aspects of individual and program aspirations, efforts, and performances are specified, measured, and shared among all, thereby enabling social comparison processes to operate. In order for sharing to take place and to provide a basis for social comparison, comparative information about individual and program plans and performances must be collected. The collection of such information is a prime feature of outcome management. Then, even without any other specific inducement to do one's best, it is expected that the exposure of oneself and one's program to one's colleagues will motivate and stimulate positive and enhanced performance.

The Principle of Action

The principle of action states that people act in order to achieve effects. It is based on Heider's (1958) postulate that the basic goal of a person is to comprehend the structure that underlies and gives rise to events. In order to know that structure and be able to capitalize on it, one must act and then perceive the effects that follow. In other words, for there to be an effect there must be an action. Therefore, a management model must require that actions occur so that effects may follow and the link between action and effect be established.

This may sound like a point whose obviousness reduces it to a state of triviality, but when one realizes how little direct action is taken in higher education management and how difficult it then becomes to link actions and effects, the meaningfulness of this point emerges. A management process must require individuals and organizations to act and to be able to perceive the effects that follow these actions. The outcome management model requires action and makes the outcomes of this action manifest.

The Principle of Intended Consequences

Closely allied to the link between action and effect is the perception that the effect is the consequence of the act and, if the act was chosen by the performer, the effect is its intended consequence. As Heider (1958) said: "There exists a hierarchy of cognitive awarenesses which begin with the more stimulus-bound recognition of 'facts' and gradually go deeper into the underlying causes of these facts" (pp. 80–81).

The principle of intended consequences might also be called the principle of instrumental behavior, after Gagne (1985), because the connection between responses and behaviors is instrumental in satisfying some motive. In other words, the action or response gets you closer to where you want to be. People, therefore, will try to identify such behaviors in advance and then carry them out because they are instrumental to goal attainment or because they intend to achieve those consequences. This principle is what gives rise to the behavior within the model that we call planning.

The Principle of Credibility

If a managerial goal is to increase the extent to which members of the public believe that an organization's product or service is good, then they must see a consistency between the organization's word and its actions. An organization whose actions are consistent with its words will be seen as credible and, therefore, will be believed. Organizations that fail to follow their own prescriptions will lose whatever influence they have because they will lose their credibility in the eyes of the public. The relationship between communicator credibility and communicator influence has been well documented by Hovland et al. (1953).

Since universities and their members often provide directions for other institutions, such as businesses, public agencies, schools, and political units, their credibility and hence their influence will depend on the extent to which they follow their own directions. Moreover, since these directions often involve the use of principles of management (such as those incorporated in our model), the continued credibility of universities and faculty may depend on their advocacy and use of the same management principles they advocate for others in operating their own academic unit. Since the university is committed to improving student outcomes, it should also be committed to improving outcomes at faculty and administrative levels.

The Principle of Rational Allocation

This principle states that resources should be given to those units that are contributing the most to the organization and taken from those that are contributing the least. This is consistent with the March and Simon (1958) idea that organizational well-being is based on maximizing the contributions of its members and on the position of Jewell and Reitz (1981) that group outcomes are dependent on group inputs.

This principle is based on the assumptions that the organization has goals and that it is important for the organization to meet its goals. To use the term coined by Allport (1962) and incorporated into an organization model by Weick (1969), we would say that the organization has a *collective structure*. The existence of and value for a group goal, over and above the sum of the individual goals, is a manifestation of a collective structure.

We might also say that the principle of rational allocation is also a principle of selective allocation aimed at reducing equivocality, to use two more of Weick's (1969) concepts. By investing resources in what works, the organization is acting selectively to move itself toward its goal, and by adopting such a rule to govern the choice process, it enables itself to make choices more unequivocally. Of course, there can be other rules for choice making and resource allocation that organizations can employ, but these would tend to be less rational or more political. Taking resources from those without political power and giving them to those with political power would be such a rule. But this would not cause the group to increase the quantity of contributions from its constituent units. Increasing subunit contributions by using them as a basis for subunit resource allocation is fundamental to the outcome management approach.

The Principle of Producer Gain

The principle of producer gain is a rational allocation rule for individuals. It states that individual rewards should be a function of individual productivity. If an organization wants to increase individual productivity, then it must reward it. If, on the other hand, rewards are distributed on a random basis or on the basis of something other than productivity, or if rewards are given equally to everybody regardless of productivity, then people will not be inclined to provide that organization with the productivity it requires to sustain itself.

According to Homans (1950), there is a reciprocal relationship between motive and activity in a social system that results in a persistence of activities that satisfy some motive. When individuals are rewarded for productive acts such as teaching or researching, those acts will be more likely to persist. Giving social recognition and material rewards for performance is posited to enhance performance.

In the outcome management model, goal-oriented behavior by organization members is a requirement not only for the organization's benefit but for the members' own benefit as well. If productive behavior by organization members benefits the organization but not the individual, then, according to both Homans (1950) and March and Simon (1958), it will not persist. Therefore, for the outcome management model to work, individual productivity must not only help the organization attain its goals (as in rational allocation) but must help the individual producer achieve his or her own goals. This means that producers must be recognized and rewarded.

The Principle of Dynamic Equilibrium

Our last principle is the one that keeps the outcome management model in motion while the parts or components remain linked. It posits that the state of the elements in the system and the relations between them are constantly changing in such a way as to keep them in a state of balance. It follows directly from the social equilibrium theory proposed by Homans (1950).

A group's goals and plans and the productivity levels of its members are always changing, but in such a way that the changes ultimately produce a state of balance. Either the goals will be achieved or they will be changed because no system can tolerate disequilibrium for an extended period of time. An unbalanced social system is like a car whose wheels are out of balance. At high speeds the vibrations can cause it to come apart.

THE MODEL

Outcome management is an approach to administration and decision making that focuses on targets or goals, called outcomes, and their attainment. The purpose of outcome management is to attain a set of goals in the quickest and most efficient manner, that is, with a minimum of both time and resources. The model is depicted in Figure 2.1. Each step in the model will be described in turn.

Figure 2.1
A Schematic of the Outcome Management Model

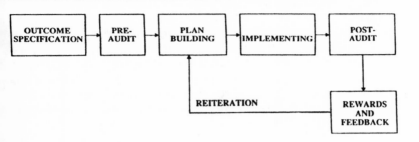

Outcome Specification

In order to attain outcomes, you must first decide what outcomes you want to attain. Within the context of organizational performance, the major outcome will usually be productivity. In higher education, productivity can be further subdivided into the triage of instructional productivity, research productivity, and service productivity. In the next two chapters, we will deal with the specifics of these three categories of productivity, but in this chapter the concepts will be presented in general terms.

The second aspect of outcome specification is the determination of how each outcome will be measured. That is the same as asking: What kind of information will I need to be able to tell how the organization is performing in a given outcome area? It is this information or these outcome measurements that will be contained within a so-called management information system.

The third and last aspect of outcome specification is the establishment of outcome criteria or benchmarks that provide a basis for determining how well or to what degree outcomes have been attained. What we are saying here is that if you are managing an organization and if you want to accomplish something you must (1) decide what that something is, (2) figure out how to measure it, and (3) determine how to judge the level of performance on it.

To use an example, let us say that you are the head of a small academic department that is being run on a shoestring and you would like to have more money available for services to faculty. The outcome you might want to achieve would be success by your faculty in obtaining contracts and grants from various external sources. The measure of that outcome would be the amount of money obtained in a year, and your criterion for success might be a quarter of a million dollars next year or, alternatively, a 20 percent increase over the amount obtained this year.

Or perhaps you are a dean who wants to be able to cover all the classes that are being offered without having either to cancel any or to ask the vice president for more money. The outcome you want to attain is total instructional coverage; your measure is the percentage of classes that you cover from your own budget, and the criterion is 100 percent.

As another example, consider a vice president who wants to enhance the prestige of his university. His outcome is the recognized quality of the academic departments as measured by rankings they achieve in national surveys, and his criterion is for half of his departments to be ranked in the top 25 in the country.

Finally, take the division director who wants as an outcome to increase each faculty member's instructional productivity. This outcome is measured by the number of student credit hours each faculty member generates with a criterion of at least 200 student credit hours per term.

Preaudit

Now that you know what you want to achieve, you need to determine how well you are currently achieving it. We call the procedure for determining your status on an outcome measure an audit, and when this comes at the beginning of an improvement sequence, we call it a preaudit. A preaudit answers the question: How well am I doing now, before I start a sequence of outcome management? In order to acquire the data or information to be included in our system, we use the auditing process.

For the external-fund-seeking department head, the preaudit takes the form of a printout of current contracts and grants. Let me see how much external money we have right now, says she, before I try anything new to improve our performance. For the dean with class coverage problems, the preaudit is his semester's record of classes covered and cost, whereas the vice president seeking prestige rushes back to old copies of *The Chronicle of Higher Education* or various published studies to discover the most recent national rankings of his departments. Meanwhile, the division director asks for class enrollment figures for the recently completed term so that she can calculate the number of student credit hours each of her faculty members generated in the classroom.

Plan Building

We are still not ready to rush out and try something new. If we wish to manage our outcomes we must have a plan for getting from where we are to where we want to be. A plan tells us what to do before we do it. It is a set of steps or a prescription for action. Football teams have game plans and teachers have lesson plans. Our department head will need a fund raising plan, our dean a scheduling plan, our vice president a quality improvement plan, and our division director either a faculty load structuring plan or a faculty development plan.

All people and organizations have resources at their disposal. A plan is a statement of intended use of those resources. Our most important individual resources are our own time and our own effort. A plan tells us how to use our time, our effort, and often the money we have at our disposal to try and achieve the level of outcomes we desire. For an organization, the major resource is the time and effort of its employees. To these are added the organization's financial resources as well as the resource of its good name.

Where does a plan come from? While occasionally we may borrow or adapt our plan from someone else's, basically our plans should come out of our own heads. You might say that plans are built out of a blend of experience and intuition. We can use other peoples' experiences in addition to our own and we can "borrow" other heads to help us with the intuition. The point to keep in mind is that if our plan does not work, we scrap it or change it.

That is our safety valve, so to speak, which protects us against a bad plan. You cannot tell how good a plan is until you try it. Just because the plan worked for the college in the next county, does not mean it will necessarily work for your college.

A plan has to be written down, and it has to be as detailed as possible. Think of the plan that a contractor uses to build a house. If a detail is missing, it can throw off the entire result.

Implementing

Now you must carry out the plan the way you have set it down on paper. When you try to carry out a step, you may discover that you need to do it somewhat differently than how you planned to do it originally. That represents a good time to change the plan, but not to abandon it altogether. You have to allow yourself some operational flexibility. You also need to have some skill in doing what the plan calls for and the motivation and determination to keep to the plan even when it calls for extra time, effort, risk, or convincing your colleagues or faculty that it will work.

You may need some help from others or some additional training or information in order to implement your plan. It is best to try to design a plan that is realistic for you and your situation so that you can implement it adequately. If you discover that your plan is more demanding than you can handle during implementation, go back to the planning step and make some reasonable changes in your plan. That is a better way to proceed than abandoning your plan altogether.

Postaudit

After you have implemented your plan, you are ready to see what you have accomplished. It is time for another contracts and grants printout, another record of classes covered, another set of national rankings, or another student credit hour analysis. If you have a management information system, it is time for another status report. In short, it is time for another audit of your performance on the outcomes you are trying to achieve. Did the plan work? Have you reached your 20 percent increment in outside funds? Have you covered all or nearly all of your classes within your budget? Have half of your departments attained national ranking? Are all of your faculty generating 200 student credit hours? The postaudit reflects the so-called bottom line. But it is your bottom line. You have set your goals, determined your baseline, set a path for improvement, and carried it out. The postaudit tells you where it has gotten you. Have you hit the bull's-eye?

Reward/Feedback

What should you do with the results of your postaudit? You may be on target, near target, or off target. There are two actions you want to take now, given the results of your efforts. First, you want to get some payoff and, second, you want to evaluate and possibly change your plan. First comes the payoff, the reward. Good effort and good results are worthy of both recognition and reward. Now that you have reached your external funding goal, buy the department a new secretary or a new microcomputer. Recommend the people who got the grants for a financial increment or a promotion. You or they are much more likely to continue the behavior that produced the desired outcome if, in so doing, there was some tangible payoff or reward. Self-satisfaction is wonderful and important but tangible payoffs go a long way toward making the necessary behavior worth doing. Give some new positions or a greater portion of the operating budget or more summer teaching opportunities to the departments that managed to cover their classes or attain national ranking or generate the desired number of student credit hours, and give the raises to the critical faculty members in each effort.

In addition to possible payoffs, outcomes also provide information. They give you feedback. They can tell you how well your plan worked. Go back over your plan and its implementation in the light of the outcomes. See what useful information you can glean about what worked and what did not work, what you could carry out and what you could not carry out.

Reiterate

Reiterate is a computer term. It means "run it again." There is always room for improvement. Take what you have learned from the postaudit and go back to step three, planning, and repeat the entire process. Perhaps you only made it to a 15 percent increase in outside funds or you covered 90 percent of your classes or a third of your departments were nationally ranked or only three-fourths of your faculty achieved 200 student credit hours. How would you go about doing it differently now? Perhaps you need to write more grant proposals or offer different courses or redistribute your budget or hire different kinds of people. You now have had a whole set of experiences to consider and reconsider in reformulating your plan and carrying it out again. Try some new wrinkles that you have discovered along the way.

Build yourself a new plan and implement it and again provide yourself and others with the rewards as appropriate. Study the feedback information again as well, so that you can consider another recycle or reiteration. By this time you may have been promoted so that external funds raised is no longer the right outcome for you. Now you can start from the very beginning and work on some new outcome such as department prestige or classes covered.

ASSETS AND LIABILITIES

It is useful to raise some questions at this point about the strengths and weaknesses of the model or what it can and cannot do for the college administrator. We will reserve our final answers to these questions to the end of the book, but we will discuss them now so that they can help you focus on and evaluate what is to follow.

In higher education, the leader or administrator does not have total control. The faculty members have partial control. The faculty members are also able to implement, follow, or coexist with any management system, but they are not necessarily willing because of possible adverse effects they believe a system might have on them. The situation a college administrator faces is one where the basic style of leadership advocated by Hersey and Blanchard (1977) would be selling, in that the administrator's basic task is to use a communication process and a social support process to get faculty members to buy into decisions that have to be made.

The outcome management system helps the administrator determine what decisions have to be made and uses rewards to get faculty members to buy into those decisions—that is, some faculty members will profit from those decisions; others will not. The principal strength of the model is that it helps tell you what decisions to make and whether they are the right decisions from a rational point of view. The principle weakness is that the model replaces certain people as the sources of influence and the recipients of resources with other people. The people replaced are those who act to maximize outcomes other than those that the administrator has set for the organization. The ones they are replaced by are those who do act to maximize the organizational outcomes.

In order to offset the liability of the model, the administrator must sell the faculty on the desired organizational goals or outcomes and thereby gain their support for and participation in the processes that must be undertaken to attain those goals. Since participating and delegating follow selling in the Hersey-Blanchard (1977) formula, we would expect faculty to help operate the outcome management model once they have been sold on the goals. (It is also likely that they may have to be sold on the idea that an academic unit or organization should even have concrete goals or that faculty members should work toward helping the organization attain those goals.)

The purpose of this book is not to show administrators how to sell organizational goals and a model for meeting them to the faculty but to show those administrators how to use that model to make decisions. However, we must point out that the selling aspect is not one that should be overlooked. Certainly, administrators should rely heavily on the two-way communication process with faculty members to explain to them how the model will result in a fair distribution of resources given their acceptance of the desired goals. In other words, if faculty members can accept or become committed to the goals, then they will receive resources based on their performance relative to those goals.

Since the goals are broad enough to cover all aspects of the accepted faculty role, all productive faculty and all productive faculty units will gain from the application of the model to the decision-making process. Moreover, all will have many opportunities to participate in its use and even steer it. Once the faculty role becomes obvious, faculty support for the model and its use should reach a level of sufficiency.

3

Specifying and Auditing Instructional Productivity

THE NEED FOR INSTRUCTIONAL PRODUCTIVITY DATA

Our interest in instructional productivity is based on the need to define an efficient teaching load for faculty members as one of our specified outcomes. The fact that some faculty members were paid an overload for teaching off campus led us to question what constituted a desirable teaching load from the organizational point of view. Some faculty members argued that since they were assigned 100 percent of their time (divided among instruction, research, and service), then any assignment beyond that should be considered an overload and paid as such. Occasionally, faculty members would be assigned to teach a course on campus, have that course canceled because of limited enrollment, have their research assignment increased, and then request overload for a course taught off campus. This seemed inefficient and counterproductive.

Justifying the denial of the request as an outcome management act required a definition of standard load. For the purpose of defining a standard or full-time load, it is sufficient to determine the average load for those members teaching in a given college during a particular term without any university-wide reference as to what that load should be. Although a standard university-wide load based on student credit hours taught per faculty member can be created (for an example of a college and university comparison, see Figure 3.1), it is seldom used for determining how much teaching should be done by individual professors in academic programs.

Figure 3.1
College of Education Instructional Efficiency Compared with University (actual 1977–85, 1986–90 Projected)

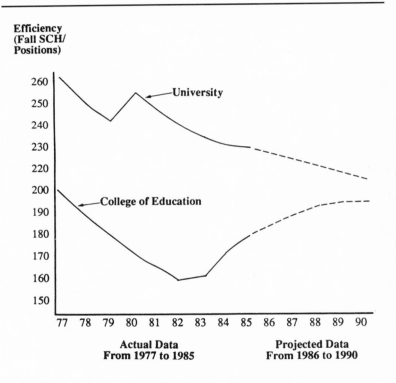

The example in Figure 3.1 uses a standard of number of student credit hours produced for each full-time equivalent faculty position for the fall term in the years 1977–85 and projects that standard to 1990. This is a measure of average productivity for each faculty member accumulated for the entire university and separately for the college of education. In our case study the average college load in 1977 turned out to be 200, which was well below the university average of 260, and continued to follow the generally downward university trend until 1982–83. Since that time the gap has narrowed and is projected to do so until 1990. This underproduction or overstaffing is reflected in most data used for our case study.

In our case study, the college average load turned out to be 270 student credit hours (SCH) per faculty member per term. Table 3.1 shows an analysis of one program. As can be seen, the nine faculty members in that program contributed five-ninths of their time to instruction and, during the term in question, produced 446 student credit hours. Had this program produced at the college average, it would have produced 1,350 student credit hours and so it was either short by some 904 student credit hours or had 3.3 too many instructional faculty. Without any attempt to seek causes for this apparent underproduction or overstaffing, it was clear that any faculty member from this program would have a difficult time justifying an overload.

Table 3.1
Teaching Loads for Faculty Members in One Program Compared to the Average College Teaching Load

Name	% INST	On-Campus SCH	Off-Campus SCH
Adams	.50	9	50
Bliss	.90	103	0
Chase	.45	0	0
Davis	.35	3	12
Edwards	.35	33	0
Franks	.75	21	26
Green	.75	36	0
Hughs	.70	69	18
Jones	.25	33	
Staff		33	82
Total	5.0	340*	106*

*Program Total = 446 SCH (Student Credit Hours)
College Average = 270 SCH per instructional FTE (Full Time Equivalent)
5 FTE x 270 SCH = 1350 SCH
1350 SCH – 446 SCH = 904 SCH below average
904 SCH / 270 SCH = 3.3 too many instructional faculty

From this initial overview of university and college teaching productivity averages as standards for overloads, it becomes clear that a data base is needed within a college so that questions of outcome attainment can be answered in a timely fashion and decisions about instructional assignments can be made.

Another view of the problem can be seen in Table 3.2. We selected 12 faculty members' loads to illustrate how high assignments of time for teaching can result in high, medium, or low productivity and also how high productivity can result from high, medium, or low teaching assignments. Differences can be reduced by some mutual agreement of just what constitutes a teaching load in terms of the number of courses and credits to be assigned to a given faculty member and what productivity is expected. For example, an 8 percent assignment can be given for each credit taught and 24 undergraduates or 18 graduates can be expected to enroll. This would balance teaching assignments with productivity.

INPUT

The first concern registered by faculty about the use of instructional productivity as a management outcome is the matter of faculty accountability. Discussions of productivity are sensitive because faculty members may associate productivity with factory work and a product as something to be marketed and sold by the institution. They may not see the number of students they teach as relative to either their teaching performance or to their contribution to the organization. However, funding agencies, legislators, and private donors require measures of productivity based on the number of students taught even when they accept all teaching as being done well. It is, therefore, essential that both the accuracy and use to which instructional productivity will be put be documented by using signed, written agreements between faculty members and the administration in order for the input to have credibility and to gain acceptance for the idea of relating the assignment of faculty time to instructional productivity measures based on the number of students taught.

Any measurement of instructional productivity also requires resolution of the question of when the data are collected. Typically,

Table 3.2
Sample of 12 Faculty Members' Teaching Loads Given Several Different Percentages of Time for Teaching

Time Given for Teaching	4 Faculty with High Productivity COURSES TAUGHT	GRADES	SCH	4 Faculty with Medium Productivity COURSES TAUGHT	GRADES	SCH	4 Faculty with Low Productivity COURSES TAUGHT	GRADES	SCH
3 High (80%) Faculty Loads	MAE 4332 (4)	33	239	EDE 5455 (3)	10	54	EVI 4222 (2)	2	23
	MAE 4816 (3)	9		EDA 5050 (3)	8		EVI 3221 (3)	5	
	MAE 4945 (10)	4					EVI 4223 (2)	2	
	MAE 4551 (2)	20							
3 Medium (65%) Faculty Loads	SCE 6761 (3)	12	357	EVI 5931 (3)	3	33	LAE 5738 (3)	8	24
	EDE 4907 (2)	27		EEX 6780 (3)	8				
	EDE 4907 (2)	18							
	SCE 4310 (3)	26							
	SCE 4310 (3)	27							
	SCE 4310 (3)	24							
3 Low (50%) Faculty Loads	EDF 5402 (4)	24	366	EDE 5306 (3)	15	45	EDA 6101 (3)	7	21
	EDF 4214 (3)	40							
	EDF 4214 (3)	50							
3 Admin and Teaching Loads	EEX 4223 (5)	18	90	LAE 5334 (3)	7	75	EVT 5800 (3)	4	16
				LAE 5333 (3)	18		EVT 5930 (1)	4	

student enrollment data come from registrars' course enrollment reports, which are sent to each department several times during a term. The most stable measure of course enrollment is the final grade report, which is sent out at the end of the semester. By this time, the course instructor has verified that each student has, in fact, taken the course, assigned the grade to each one of the students, and signed the grade reporting form. For some uses, these data might be a bit late, but data captured earlier are likely to be judged unreliable and invalid by faculty members.

If all staff support personnel and computers worked when and as they were supposed to, it would be a relatively easy matter to capture all of the data required for an instructional productivity analysis from a computer program written and implemented by the registrar. Unfortunately, our experience in the case study indicated that this was impractical. The registrar was too busy getting out final grades and worrying about commencement to have time to worry about instructional productivity analyses conducted by individual academic units.

The data we did receive were actually accompanied by a note to verify them with the academic department. Our solution was to ask the department secretary to take selected information from the final grade roster at the time the faculty member turned in the signed grade sheets. Even in large departments, we found it took relatively little time, was comparatively error-free, and that this simple procedure made the desired data available to us immediately after each academic term. The form itself, shown in Figure 3.2, is called the Faculty Activity—Current Term or F.A.C.T. Sheet.

The F.A.C.T. Sheet requires the department head to assign the level of the course, the number of credits, and the number of students expected to receive grades. At the end of the term, actual student numbers are entered, and the department head verifies on each form the percentage of time that has been assigned to instruction, research, service, or other administrative duties. The names of graduate advisees are maintained as an ongoing part of the F.A.C.T. system on a 1–2–3 Lotus spreadsheet that each academic department uses to update its individual part of the system. All personnel reporting (PARS) for the entire academic year is done on a disc with a single data entry.

Figure 3.2
Form for Collecting Data on Individual Faculty Member Instructional Productivity per Term (F.A.C.T. Sheet)

FACULTY ACTIVITY - CURRENT TERM

NAME   TERM

F.T.E.F.

_____%

Assigned Inst._____% Research_____% Service_____%

Fixed Credit Courses

Prefix   Section   Credits   #Grades Given

Variable Credit Courses

Prefix   Section   Student Names & (Credits)

Major Professor for: Name (degree)

The system described above has the virtue of including (1) the faculty assignment, which is signed by both the faculty member and the department head, (2) the official grade roster, which is signed by the department head and the faculty member, and (3) the assignment of advisees, which is also signed by the faculty member and the department head. While it rarely may be necessary to produce the actual written documents that provide the productivity data, it is important to the credibility of the data that they originate from written agreement by the parties involved.

PROCESS (THE MANAGEMENT INFORMATION SYSTEM)

The analytic process of instructional productivity involves the identification of variables that represent basic elements of productivity, and the description of how the elements relate to each other. From the basic data contained on the F.A.C.T. Sheet, the variables found in Table 3.3 can be calculated and divided for levels of instruction, types of courses, ranks of instructors, major and nonmajor instruction, and so on.

Table 3.3 represents the basic management system information across individual faculty members. The demographics on each faculty member includes an identification number, race, sex, rank (1 = instructor, 2 = assistant professor, 3 = associate professor, 4 = professor) year of employment (YOE), and year of birth (YOB). The assignment for each term is divided into the percentage of instruction (%INST), research (%RSH), and service (%SERV). The specific performance in instruction and advisement for the term is divided into undergraduate student credit hours (UG SCH), graduate student credit hours (GR SCH), and number of PhD advisees (PHD). The specific research and service activities (which are germane to the next chapter) cover a five-year period and include number of articles (JOUR), number of presentations at national meetings (PRES), number of contracts and grants in force (CONT), and number of written but unpublished research reports (REPT). Finally, the salary data include MERIT pay, total SALARY, and merit pay divided by salary (M/SAL).

The basic objective of a management information system for managing desired outcomes is to process only those data elements that are related directly to final productivity measures. If this can be done, it would indicate that the computerized system was as

Table 3.3
Productivity Data by Selected Individual Faculty Member Within the Management Information System

Demographics						Assignment			Instruction			Research*				Salary**		
NUMBER	RANK	RACE	SEX	YOE	YOB	%INST	%RSH	%SERV	UG SCH	GR SCH	PHD	JOUR	PRES	CONT	REPT	MERIT	SALARY	M/SAL
52442	3	1	1	63	25	75	10	15	75	15	0	2	0	0	2	7.46	281	26
52447	4	1	1	68	38	80	10	10	140	14	1	30	0	0	13	15.01	358	41
52445	3	1	1	71	42	40	45	15	39	1	0	5	2	2	0	11.61	301	38
52426	3	1	1	71	42	50	25	25	24	0	0	0	0	0	0	0.81	224	3
52436	4	1	1	61	21	60	20	20	93	79	1	3	0	0	0	18.64	384	48
52429	4	1	2	83	40	55	25	20	27	63	1	0	5	0	1	8.89	317	28
52410	4	1	1	74	40	60	15	25	0	67	3	0	0	1	1	8.44	328	25
52417	4	1	1	69	18	30	50	20	0	7	0	11	3	0	0	9.59	317	30
52443	4	1	1	71	42	85	5	10	0	61	6	3	11	0	0	10.29	317	32
52425	4	1	1	56	21	65	25	10	36	3	1	1	0	0	0	9.45	404	23
52396	4	1	1	68	24	80	10	10	166	12	2	0	0	1	0	4.60	334	13
52446	4	1	1	70	29	55	35	10	0	81	2	2	1	0	0	13.34	441	30
52437	4	1	1	66	34	20	25	55	0	3	0	4	10	1	0	2.93	281	10
52423	4	1	1	56	23	70	15	10	108	14	2	2	19	0	0	7.34	441	16
52434	4	1	1	62	31	85	0	1	227	24	1	7	0	0	2	13.93	397	35
52397	4	1	1	67	30	85	10	5	194	47	1	3	6	0	1	5.13	306	16
52533	4	1	1	66	32	70	20	10	0	25	2	0	8	4	1	12.65	397	31

*This will be covered in the next Chapter.
**This will be covered in Chapter 8.

efficient as possible. This level of efficiency proved to be unattainable in actual practice within the case study. As selected variables entered into the system, new variables were suggested from those selected and new questions were raised, based on the information provided by the variables initially identified. For example, when we identified students by major programs, the question arose as to whether the productivity should be associated with the instructor's department offering the course or whether the productivity should be associated with the major in which the student was enrolled. The answer to this question required the generation of a matrix so we could access the collegewide impact. Our original data base needed to be revised to answer other questions at a more sophisticated level.

The recommended data processing for instructional productivity is to keep the basic data elements in the simple form of the F.A.C.T Sheet and use off-the-shelf software packages, which are now readily available (for example, Lotus or Symphony) to do microcomputer analyses, once possible only on mainframe computers. Additionally, the software packages provide the flexibility to answer more complicated questions with more sophisticated software without major modifications in the data base. A summary of instructional productivity of all programs in the case study college appears in Table 3.4.

Table 3.4 represents the basic management information system for programs and is formed by accumulating data across individual faculty members (see Table 3.3) based on the F.A.C.T. Sheets. For each program the total number of faculty positions for fall 1985 in the form of full-time equivalent faculty (FTEF) is given and then divided into the percentages assigned for INSTruction, ReSearCH, and SERVice, respectively. Data are then provided for the number of FIXed Student Credit Hours (SCH) for UPPer division, LOWer division, and GRADuate credits. The number of VARiable credit STudents and CRedits are added to yield the TOTal Student Credit Hours for the fall 1985 term. Finally, the number of PHD CANDidates and the dissertation CRedits they took are recorded. This covers all the necessary management information in the area of instruction distributed across programs.

The most useful analyses of instructional productivity should begin with clearly stated questions that need to be answered in order to manage an outcome, that is, to make a decision or take

Table 3.4

Instructional Productivity Data by Program Within the Management Information System

DEPARTMENT	Program	F85% FTE	F85% INST	F85% RSCH	F85% SERV	FIX STU	SCH GRAD	SCH UPP	SCH LOW	VAR STU	VAR CR	TOT SCH	PHD CAND	PHD CR
A	19	4.00	2.45	1.00	0.55	144	110	215		9	23	348	4	14
	11	7.50	5.10	1.15	1.25	475	335	1028		9	16	1379	4	7
	22	1.00	0.50	0.25	0.25	71		130		1	3	133		
	Non-Faculty					162	5	2752				2757		
		12.50	**8.05**	**2.40**	**2.05**	**852**	**450**	**4125**		**19**	**42**	**4617**	**8**	**21**
B	20	0.50	0.35	0.10	0.05	23		69		4	21	90	3	21
	18	3.50	1.85	0.45	1.20	89	72	248		12	30	350	5	10
	4	6.00	4.00	1.20	0.80	163	62	557		48	65	684	2	6
	9	5.00	3.65	0.75	0.60	74	191	102		39	101	394	12	32
	Non-Faculty					117	198	214		1	3	415		
		15.00	**9.85**	**2.50**	**2.65**	**466**	**523**	**1190**		**104**	**220**	**1933**	**22**	**69**
C	2	11.00	7.00	1.45	2.55	192	546			32	72	618	41	92
	8	6.50	3.50	1.70	1.20	135	381			47	92	473	28	70
	14	2.50	1.25	0.95	0.30	39	101			16	24	125	9	23
	16	5.00	3.65	0.75	0.60	89	234			29	71	305	17	52
		25.00	**15.40**	**4.85**	**4.65**	**455**	**1262**			**124**	**259**	**1521**	**95**	**237**

(continued)

Table 3.4 (continued)

D	6	10.00	3.50	3.95	2.55	246	812	24		37	85	921	21	62
	7	7.50	3.45	2.80	1.25	360	496	486		22	63	1045	9	33
	5	7.00	3.00	3.00	1.00	328	344	552		25	68	964	18	49
	Non-Faculty					34	112			5	11	123	1	1
		24.50	**9.95**	**9.75**	**4.80**	**968**	**1764**	**1062**		**89**	**227**	**3053**	**49**	**145**
E	10	5.75	3.70	0.75	1.30	187	434	120		48	135	689	16	54
	17	3.00	2.25	0.35	0.40	67	193			15	405	598	3	15
	13	4.50	2.83	0.70	0.97	336	42	1230		3	9	1281		
	21	2.00	1.35	0.25	0.40	66	126	102		7	16	244		
	Non-Faculty						51	998				1049		
		15.25	**10.13**	**2.05**	**3.07**	**656**	**846**	**2450**		**73**	**565**	**3861**	**19**	**69**
F	1	9.25	6.45	1.25	1.55	519	261	1123		42	130	1553	8	26
	15	5.00	3.35	0.75	0.90	238	286	462	39	23	61	809	2	13
	Non-Faculty					734		146	670			816		
		14.25	**9.80**	**2.00**	**2.45**	**1491**	**547**	**1731**	**709**	**65**	**191**	**3178**	**10**	**39**
G	12	5.50	3.65	0.85	1.00	55	208			7	23	231	7	23
	3	10.00	6.50	1.10	2.40	229	236	684		62	287	1207	6	21
	Non-Faculty					136	96	368				464		
		15.50	**10.15**	**1.95**	**3.40**	**420**	**540**	**1052**		**69**	**310**	**1902**	**13**	**44**
COLLEGE	Total	**122.00**	**73.33**	**25.50**	**23.07**	**5308**	**5932**	**11610**	**709**	**543**	**1814**	**20065**	**216**	**624**

an action. Among the most common questions to ask is the one at the beginning of this chapter: Is the work load for the academic unit evenly distributed among faculty members? The answer, typically, is not a simple matter of numbers, but rather is influenced by (1) the level at which the course is taught, (2) whether the course is a survey course for majors and nonmajors or a specialized course exclusively for majors, and (3) whether the course involves a great deal of instructor time working with individual students (statistics, for example) or whether the course accommodates a large number of students in a lecture hall. The answers to these questions need to be translated into a measure of capacity that represents the total possible number of full-time equivalent faculty and the number of student credit hours involved.

The F.A.C.T. Sheet lists the percentage of time devoted to instruction, and from this the number of faculty required to teach can be calculated. Student credit hours (SCH), which equals number of students in a course times number of credits taken, is also easily calculated from the form. Next, for budgetary purposes, a hypothetical full-time equivalent student (FTES) can be created by taking the number of credits a student typically took in a term (12 credits at the graduate level and 15 credits at the undergraduate) and dividing it into the number of student credit hours. Finally, salary dollars ought to be considered in an analysis of faculty productivity since faculty salary, while determined more by the rank and experience over all level of courses taught and number of students involved (see Chapter 8), does provide some insight into the use of resources.

Figure 3.3 shows the instructional cost for each of the 22 programs in the college of education case study and is calculated by dividing enrollments in each program by the combined salaries of the faculty in the program. From Figure 3.3, it is clear that programs vary widely in what they cost the institution.

Other kinds of questions can be answered using the basic F.A.C.T. Sheet. The flexibility of the spreadsheet allows for rapid ordering of faculty by age to plan the impact of impending retirements. Salaries can be looked at by ordering the percentage of pay raises to see if any potential race or gender bias needs to be investigated further. Fluctuations in enrollments can be traced to see if some form of flexible contract may meet students' needs

Figure 3.3
Cost per Student Credit Hour for Each of the 22 Programs

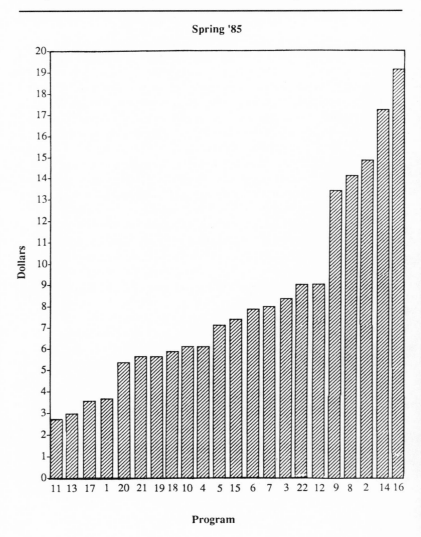

Spring '85

Dollars

Program

more effectively. Graduate student advising loads may be screened to see if any programs have large numbers of inactive students assigned to faculty members as a part of their total load. There are many combinations of data that suggest problems or opportunities and require additional study.

OUTPUT

Data on the outputs of instructional productivity usually come from three sources. Whenever possible, rely on permanent records that contain the basic data in an unaccumulated form. Typically, those reports provided by the first source, the business office, include (1) head count of faculty by rank, (2) head count of faculty be degree, (3) faculty load (which divides the faculty member's time into teaching, research, and service), (4) average faculty salaries by rank for both the academic year and the summer term, (5) budgets for the academic year and summer term coming from institutional funds (including dollars spent for instructional faculty, research faculty, service faculty, college and department administration, support personnel, graduate assistants, personal fringe benefits, operating expenses and capital outlay), and (6) the same kinds of data as in the fifth category accumulated for contracts and grants.

The second source, the registrar, provides data on the credit hour production for the academic year and summer session collected at the undergraduate, beginning graduate, and advance graduate levels and specifies the number of course sections taught, the class enrollments, and the student credit hours. The final permanent report from the graduate office, the third source, contains information on the number of graduates in a given academic year, including summer session at the bachelor's, master's, and doctorate levels. These data are recorded each year and stored in the computer system, so they are available to examine trend data and to compare productivity from year to year.

Data from permanent records can be supplemented with basic information from F.A.C.T. Sheets in order to complete an analysis on a specific question. Such questions might include: How successful have we been in meeting our projected enrollment at several levels over the past few years? How nearly does our cost per student credit hour match the cost per student credit hours at comparable institutions? Are we providing funding in the summer session to support student programs or faculty research? It is difficult to anticipate what these questions will be, but it is important to be able to bring data to bear on these issues as soon as they arise.

The clearest demonstration of how student credit hours can be used to identify problems of expenditures across programs or departments is seen when one looks at the allocation of monies for a summer term. The summer term is somewhat different from the regular academic year in that the monies expended during the summer are used to pay directly for student credit hours and not for research assignments or service commitments. One of the underlying assumptions of a summer term funded primarily for teaching courses is that a student credit hour should cost as much in one program as it does in another, so that once a college average is established, there should not be a great deal of variation from that average.

In Table 3.5 we see the faculty salary dollars allocated to each of seven programs in the college of education case study, the full-time equivalent students produced from those dollars, a division of the students produced by the faculty salaries, and the net loss or gain. It can be seen, further, that if one were to allocate approximately the same number of dollars in the following summer, two departments would need to be reduced about 3 percent each and those salary dollars given to two more productive departments in order to achieve equity as a consequence of the management outcome of degree of instructional productivity.

CONCLUSION

The input, process, and output of instructional productivity data are much more flexible today than they have been in the past decade. The microcomputer has allowed institutions to share data at many levels and to allow individual academic units to do their own analyses in order to try to understand the problems and issues associated with instructional productivity. The availability of software packages that can be shared among the academic units and the dedication of personnel exclusively to data processing and statistical analysis within the academic unit have greatly facilitated

Table 3.5
An Analysis of the Return on Summer Session Budget Allocations for the Preceding Summer and Its Application to Planning for the Succeeding Summer

Dept	Sum of Faculty Salaries	Analysis of Preceding Summer No of Full-Time Equivalent Students (FTES)	Salaries : FTES	Over/under Funding*
B	$49,981	50	$1,00	+$22,000
C	108,920	175	622	+13,000
College	399,888	727	550	0
E	64,420	118	546	-1,000
D	81,792	160	511	-4,000
G	29,166	60	486	-6,000
F	32,606	77	423	-9,000
A	33,021	87	380	-15,000

Dept	Plan for Succeeding Summer Approx new Allocation	% of Total	% Change
B	$35,000	9	-3
C	95,000	24	-3
E	65,000	16	0
D	85,000	21	0
G	30,000	7	0
F	40,000	10	+2
A	50,000	13	+4
College	400,000	100	0

* Approximate amount of excess or shortage in funding that if adjusted for, would put the department at the same salary per FTES level as the College as a whole.

the decentralization of analysis and decision making within academic institutions. It is somewhat ironic that some faculty members hold a mechanistic and bureaucratic perception of a management information system when it is precisely the tool that allows faculty members to share more widely in the decision-making process. Far from being a tool of central control, the microcomputer and the attendant software have become agents for democratizing academic institutions in the decision-making process.

4

Accounting for Academic Research and Service

DEFINITIONAL PROBLEMS

Academic research and service activities are defined here as any activities carried out by faculty members during the time allocated to research or service and reported on the faculty members' assignment forms for a given term. This definition is obviously circular and does not contain operational statements of what faculty members are doing during the research or service time.

There are two reasons for this. In the first place, it is difficult for faculty members to know, at the time they are engaged in a given hour of research or service, whether that hour will result in a product. Second, faculty members often hold contracts to develop specific products to provide a service, but the development process requires time to complete and may include research activities that yield published journal articles as a product, in addition to the product contracted for.

Finally, because it is difficult to draw fine lines between research and service activities, at the very least one can view all research and service activities as noninstructional. This combination and its assessment seem reasonable since it accounts for 30 percent of the assignment (the other 70 percent being instruction). Nevertheless, faculty members do receive greater rewards for their research (promotion, merit pay, external support for graduate assistants, travel) and greater personal rewards from service (consulting fees, travel, professional recognition) than they receive for teaching. Faculty members are, therefore, motivated to devote as much time as possible to these noninstructional activities.

Administrators who are concerned with providing resources view research and service activities as nonproductive in the sense that instructional productivity is the base for funding. These administrators need to be assured that noninstructional assignments have at least the potential to increase resources. Without some potential resources from research and service products, the administrator tends to assign faculty members a larger instructional responsibility. This decision runs the risk of lowered responsiveness to external needs, reduced recognition for the institution (two of our institutional goals), and consequently, diminished ability to compete for high-quality external funds.

This point was illustrated in April 1985 when a consortium of 39 schools of education, called the Dean's Network, published a report of studies supported by the Ford Foundation on advanced graduate programs in education (Brown, 1985). The college of education used in the case study was included in the Brown report, along with other large land-grant institutions and large private schools like Harvard, Northwestern, and Stanford. Each of the 39 schools of education in the study was placed on one of four levels according to its performance on measures of faculty, students, and programs. The greatest quality difference occurred between the second- and third-level institutions. The college of education in the case study was in the lowest level, primarily because of the relatively small amount of time its faculty members were given for research activities.

The number of publications in refereed journals, the basic quality measure of the Brown study, was greater for first- and second-level institutions, but the publication rate was equal when the number of publications was weighted by the time assigned for research. This weighting removed most of the differences among levels. Consoling as that may have been, the weighting did not help the college of education in the case study in national ratings where absolute number of publications is the major criterion. The

distribution of faculty time assigned to research for the 39 schools
when compared to the time assignment at the case study college
is found in Table 4.1 and the comparative publication rates are
found in Table 4.2.

Table 4.1
Distribution of Time Assigned for Research

Number	39 Schools	Case Study College
0 - 1	25	45
2 - 3	22	16
4 - 8	30	26
9 +	23	13

Table 4.2
Number of Publications in Refereed Journals in Last Five Years

% of Time Assigned to Research	% of Faculty: 39 Schools Average	% of Faculty: Case Study College Total
0 - 5	25.3	17.4
6 - 25	44.4	63.6
26 - 50	25.4	19.0
51 - 75	4.0	0
76 - 100	.9	0

It can be seen from the tables that both the time allocated for
research and the journal publication rate of the college of education
in the case study are somewhat lower than the average of these
39 schools. From Table 4.3, it can be seen that number of publications is related to the time assigned for research. The college

will need to monitor the data in Table 4.3 to be sure that faculty members who are publishing in refereed journals have reduced teaching loads and those who have reduced loads continue to publish. In other words, a distinction must be made between time allocated for research and research productivity, but the fact that the two measures are related must also be considered.

Table 4.3
Comparison of the Input of Assigned Research Time and the Output of Number of Journal Publications

Input: % of Assigned Research Time	Output: Total 5 year Journal Publications	Output: % Faculty Publishing	Output: 5 year Average of Publishing Faculty
0 - 5	47	50	4.7
6 - 25	242	69	4.6
26 - 50	96	78	5.3
51 - 75	0	0	0
76 - 100	0	0	0

PRODUCTIVITY MEASURES

Accounting for academic research and services is a long-term effort that requires regular attention to be focused on trends toward and away from some general goals. In the case study, the college goals relevant to research and service were efficient use of resources to provide responsiveness to the needs of the profession and the society it serves, and recognition for the efforts. Institutional research provided data on research assignments, quantity and quality of publications, current research activity, career research productivity, and merit and other discretionary pay incentives.

In the college of education case study, we began with data taken from the faculty Research Assignment Proposals (described in

Chapter 6) to determine the amount and kinds of research activities in which faculty are involved. The results of this analysis are shown in Table 4.4.

The rough analysis in Table 4.4 shows an active faculty with an average of 3.5 research activities per faculty member and an average productivity of 3.0 products per faculty member for the year studied. Rather than focus exclusively on any one index of research productivity at this point, data are reported separately for a wide number of indicators.

Table 4.4
Summary of Research Assignment Proposal Data for the Entire Case Study College of Education Faculty (Excluding Administrators) for the Last Academic Year

Activities in which faculty are involved*	N
Research (collection of data, etc.)	179
Scholarly activity (other than research)	218
Consulting	14
Programmatic	55

Anticipated products	N
Grant proposals	21
Articles	192
Monographs	21
Books	41
Program activity	
a. Clinics/counseling/testing	16
b. Workshops/conferences	18
c. Conference proceedings	6
d. Curriculum materials	11
e. Reports to governments committees/agencies	42
f. Test instruments/integrated reports	2
Speeches/Papers/Reports	
a. Presentation of papers at conventions	27
b. Presentation of reports to government	2
c. Editing	2
Service to Community	7

* The number of faculty in this analysis was 134 and approximately 16% of their collective load was devoted to research each semester with one quarter of that paid for by external funds.

To determine what research productivity looked like over a longer time frame than a single year, especially since a research project cannot be conceived, completed, and reported in so short a time, an analysis was made of the research productivity of faculty over a five-year period. (For this analysis, only faculty who were online full time for all five years were included.) The results of this analysis are shown in Table 4.5. Again, as in the one-year analysis, there is considerable evidence of wide-ranging productivity on a broad number of indicators.

However, to create a data base for productivity that is likely to result in the organization meeting its goal of national recognition,

Table 4.5
Five-Year Averages for Research Productivity*

Product	Mean Number	Standard Deviation
Publication in refereed journal	1.9	4.6
Publication in non-ref. journal	2.4	2.8
Research publication**	1.6	2.4
Scholarly publication**	2.5	3.7
Creative publication**	1.1	2.4
Book publication	1.0	3.3
Monograph publication	0.8	1.6
Presentation of paper	6.8	12.0
Unpublished report	3.0	4.6
Contract	0.4	0.7
National leadership role	0.2	0.5
State leadership role	0.1	0.4

*The number of faculty for this analysis was 83, these being the subset of the total faculty who were present and on-line on a full-time basis for all five years studied.

**Research=date-based (empirical); Scholarly=theoretical, discursive, review; Creative=developmental, instructional.

we must focus on research products that contribute directly to this goal. The research product that was deemed most effective in maximizing the recognition outcome was the publication, because of its perceived authenticity and potentially national distribution. We chose to build a management information system to use in monitoring performances relative to the recognition outcome, to use number of publications as the basic indicator, to accumulate data by program over a five-year time span, and to include performances by all faculty (regardless of discontinuity) using the program as the unit of analysis.

In considering the publication as the research performance indicator, we continued to distinguish between publications in refereed journals and those in nonrefereed journals, and to report both, with the perception that the former was a better indicator of quality than the latter. We also distinguished among three categories of publication type: (1) research publication, meaning the publication of a data-based or empirical study; (2) scholarly publication, meaning the publication of a theoretical or discursive piece, such as a review article; and (3) creative publication, meaning the publication of a developmental or instructional piece, such as a manual. We made no qualitative distinctions among these types, although the research type was the most likely to appear in a refereed source.

The basic management information system for research productivity appears in Table 4.6. It includes all faculty by program and spans five years. It reveals that although 90 percent of the faculty in the case study had produced a publication during this time span, only about one-third were in refereed journals and fewer than one-third were of the research or data-based type. It also reveals wide variations in research productivity by program and department. Note the high productivity by all three programs in department D (an average of about one refereed publication per faculty member per year) compared to the low productivity by all four programs in department C (an average of about one refereed publication per faculty member per five years). The 5:1 ratio between departments in research productivity on this one measure would have great implications for decisions about allocation of funds for research support.

It is also helpful to know how active faculty members have been

Table 4.6
Analysis of Faculty of Education Publications over a Five-Year Period (1980–85)

Dept.	Program	# of Faculty	% of Faculty who Publish	Number of Publications by Type*			Total # Publ.	# of Refereed	% of Refereed+
				Research	Scholarly	Creative			
A**	19	4	100	10	16	30	56	21	33
	11	8	50	6	40	25	71	26	50
	22	2	50	14	4	10	28	12	50
	12	10	90	24	17	10	51	16	40
	3	6	90	20	13	7	40	20	20
Total A		**30**	**80**	**74**	**90**	**82**	**246**	**95**	**38**
B	20	2	100	7	7	3	17	0	0
	18	4	100	13	21	32	66	24	19
	4	8	100	23	20	31	74	13	20
	9	14	100	6	13	15	34	9	30
Total B		**19**	**100**	**49**	**61**	**81**	**191**	**46**	**24**
C	2	14	30	0	14	6	20	2	0
	8	8	40	12	13	9	34	13	20
	4	4	80	11	11	6	28	9	33
	5	5	100	8	31	8	47	16	20
Total C		**31**	**71**	**31**	**69**	**29**	**129**	**40**	**23**

D	6	8	100	16	56	18	90	56	53
	7	9	100	44	70	8	122	33	40
	5	8	100	24	53	11	87	42	42
Total D		**25**	**100**	**84**	**179**	**37**	**299**	**131**	**44**
E	10	12	100	42	18	2	62	9	40
	17	4	100	28	22	13	63	25	60
	13	5	100	1	13	13	27	4	20
	21	2	100	1	14	7	22	12	50
Total E		**23**	**100**	**72**	**67**	**35**	**174**	**50**	**52**
F	1	12	75	20	51	21	92	15	30
	15	4	100	32	30	4	66	11	25
Total F		**16**	**81**	**52**	**81**	**25**	**158**	**26**	**28**
College Total		**144**	**90**	**362**	**547**	**289**	**1197**	**388**	**36**

* R=Research (analysis of original data); S=Scholarship (development of a theoretical direction or review of findings); C=Creativity (curriculum development, training, miscellaneous).

** At the start of the case study, Department A and G were a single department, labeled "A."

+ Publications in journals which require review by "referees."

over a five-year period in leadership positions in the professional associations at the state and national levels, since these activities, although appearing to be of a service nature, contribute primarily to the goal of recognition. Such an analysis for the case study college of education appears in Table 4.7. This analysis shows that about two-thirds of the case study college faculty have played a leadership role in national or state associations. Considering the rather small percentage of time devoted to these activities, that record looks good.

Certainly, we would want to maintain such a record of national and state leadership efforts by individual faculty as a part of our management information system so that we could reward such efforts as contributing to organizational goal attainment.

Table 4.7
Description and Listing of Faculty Serving in Leadership Roles* in National and State Professional Organizations

Department	National		State	
	Number	Percent	Number	Percent
A	18	60	17	56
B	8	42	7	37
C	22	71	22	71
D	20	80	13	52
E	15	65	14	61
F	11	69	13	81
Total	**94**	**65**	**86**	**60**

*Examples of leadership roles:
   President, National Association of Biology Teachers
   Director of Research & Study Grants, American Association of Colleges of Teacher Education
   President, Association for Education of the Visually Handicapped
   Chair of Committee on Migratory Children and Reading, International Reading Association
   Chair of Advisory Committee, National Council for Social Studies
   Chair of Outstanding Dissertation Award Committee, Council on the Teaching of Foreign Languages

DEFINING SERVICE PRODUCTIVITY

Most of the noninstructional productivity discussed in this chapter thus far has focused on research. Research produces such products as publications and reports or contracts and grants, and, as we have seen earlier in this chapter, these products can be classified and counted. A classifiable and quantifiable product is a sine qua non for a management information system. When it comes to the area of service, the third prong of the traditional university trinity, it is not clear nor obvious what kinds of products should be counted.

It is possible to consider service in the sense of service to one's profession with the major manifestation or product being the assumption of a leadership role in a professional association. (This approach has already been briefly discussed and described and, although not appropriate to research productivity, it does seem to contribute more to recognition than to responsiveness.) Or, alternatively, service could be regarded as contributions to national efforts in one's professional specialty such as serving on national commissions. However, there would not be enough instances of this occurrence to make it a practical measure.

A third way to view service might be consultations in the field such as education faculty working with public schools, business faculty working with local business enterprises, public administration faculty working with public agencies, and so on. The problem with this conception of service is that it would be limited primarily to the faculty of professional schools for whom a clear linkage to a specific field exists. It would be hard to evaluate the service contributions of a philosophy professor, for example.

A fourth view of service might be in terms of service to one's own organization through such acts as serving on committees or accepting other assignments that benefit the organization (such as going on recruiting trips or being available on parents' weekends).

One way to resolve the problem of what constitutes service is to view it in terms of the outcome management model around which this book is organized. The outcomes to be measured in higher education, according to outcome management theory, are defined in terms of the organizational goals of which they are measured. One set of outcomes will be chosen because they reflect or contribute to recognition of the institution by the profession, while another set of outcomes will be important because they represent responsive contributions by the institution to public need. Presumed service activities such as holding leadership roles in professional organizations are more likely to contribute to the goal of recognition than to the goal of responsiveness. Research, as well, is an outcome that will enhance recognition more so than reflect responsiveness. Both research and professional leadership roles have already been presented as noninstructional outcomes.

In terms of meeting the goal of responsiveness, we can identify three activities that may reasonably qualify. In the order of their appropriateness, they are

- Direct assistance to a field-based unit
- Applied research (i.e., research done in a field-based unit)
- Direct assistance to one's own organization

Consultations

Direct assistance to a field-based unit can take many forms but they would mostly all be considered consultations. Such consultations would be on-site attempts to help a field-based unit solve its problems or improve its operations through diagnosis, advisement, or training. In the college of education case study, consultations typically dealt with public school administration, program design, curriculum, teaching, or student services. Some specific examples include the following:

- Developing and field-testing a statewide writing test
- Training state education agency personnel in the skills development approach to bilingual education
- Developing a set of science objectives and test items for use by the high school science teachers of the state
- Evaluating Homestead School District's second grade reading program
- Training fifth grade teachers in Statesville to integrate reading and writing instruction

- Disseminating instructional materials to vocational teachers statewide
- Serving on the local school district's management development council
- Interviewing prospective administrators for county schools
- Designing and implementing an instructional program in basic mathematics for low achieving students in Scarlett County
- Operating a daily exercise program for local elderly people
- Serving on the advisory committee for the local area agency for the aging

Consultations for local, state, national, and even international organizations, agencies, and companies may provide the faculty member serving as the consultant with remunerative gain or not, and may also serve as the basis for a published article or report or not. From an outcome management perspective, the only matter of importance is that such activities, all of which can be considered to be responsive in nature to external need, take place.

There is, however, also the matter of keeping track of such activities so that instances can be recorded and reported as evidence of responsive organizational behavior. This can be accomplished using the Service Assignment Plan and Service Assignment Report described in Chapter 6.

Applied Research

Applied research represents a much grayer area than consultations in the measurement and specification of service productivity. This is so because it is often difficult to separate research from applied research, particularly in the professional disciplines, such as education, business, engineering, law, and the like. Equally true is the fact that applied research may result in a journal publication and hence be counted twice, once as a research product and once as a service product.

In the college of education case study, applied research efforts had titles such as the following:

- A study of the commitment of college-aged adults to the normative values of the culture and its implication for the K–12 curriculum
- Questioning behavior of young children and its relation to the learning of science
- A study of the effectiveness of two computerized teaching programs
- A study to determine why disadvantaged students tend to select low-level vocational programs
- A study of the vocational skills required for attaining journeyman-level competency
- A longitudinal analysis of reading comprehension scores as a basis for diagnosis and treatment of reading difficulties
- The effects of acute physical exercise on the state anxiety and mental performance of women business executives

It is entirely likely that any of the above projects that resulted in journal publications were counted as research products. It may, however, not be unreasonable to count studies such as these twice, both as research and service, if they contribute to both recognition and responsiveness goals.

Organizational Assistance

In order to operate and maintain itself as an organization, there are many task that an organization's members must carry out. Performing such tasks may not help the members individually, but they may be of critical value to the organization. On the other end of the continuum, there are individual member activities that require inordinate amounts of administrator time to deal with (such as unprofessional, illegal, and immoral acts).

It is hard to quantify activities that contribute to organizational governance and success and those that detract from it. Some faculty members serve on large numbers of committees, but these are committees that accomplish little, whereas other faculty members may serve on one committee, but it is critical in its contributions. Some faculty members use committee membership as a means of blocking the organization from meeting its goals, or as a means of expanding their own political power base for personal gain.

Then there are a whole host of activities that help an organization that have nothing to do with formal committee structure or function. These are often in response to impromptu opportunities for recruiting of students or performing other public relations functions. Some faculty members will almost always be available for such assignments, while others will not. Rarely is it practical or even possible to record all of these occurrences.

In Chapter 8, we discuss a rating system for measuring and accounting for service in the form of organizational assistance. It is based on administrator judgment rather than on quantifiable events such as research publications, consultations, or student credit hours taught, and so it is likely to be suspect by some. However, it does represent one, albeit imperfect, way to ensure that individual assistance to the organization becomes a matter of record and a basis for reward.

5

The Planning Process

The planning process can be seen as the sum of all the steps in outcome management by the individuals who are carrying it out. Ideally, the planning process should be carried out by faculty members in increasingly larger numbers in order to arrive at consensus. The basic purpose of the planning process is to decide on the allocation of resources among all of the units of the organization.

As was done in the preceding chapters, the academic program area will again be used as the basic management unit. Goal sharing should be greatest among faculty members who work in a common program area because of their overlapping interests and expertise and the academic directions of their students. Programs can then be cumulated into departments and departments cumulated into schools or colleges.

CONSTRUCTING OUTCOME OBJECTIVES

In order to begin the planning process, each program must determine its own plan based on its own desired outcomes. Hence, the first step in the planning process is for each program to construct a set of outcome objectives. Examples of what such outcome

objectives might be are as follows: increasing (1) number of students, (2) students' level of performance or capability, (3) faculty
productivity, (4) faculty morale, (5) program recognition, (6) program responsiveness to the needs of the field, (7) department efficiency, and (8) department quality of management (called
sufficiency).

For purposes of practicality, it is recommended that no program
develop or submit more than five outcome objectives. The reasons
for this are that (1) it is difficult, if not impossible, for members
of a program faculty to put in the time and effort to pursue a larger
number of objectives; (2) it is rare to be able to give a program
sufficient resources to fund more than five; and (3) planning for
more than five objectives may cause the critical goals to be ob-
scured. Therefore, the objectives should be presented in order of
priority so that a number fewer than five can be pursued if personnel or financial resources are in short supply and so that the
most important ones will stand out.

Below are some illustrative examples of outcome objectives for
a variety of program areas:

- Increase the impact on human service agencies by adding
  additional programs (special education)
- Increase enrollment at the doctoral level by means of a
  weekend program (public administration)
- Increase the proficiency in educational measurement and
  testing skills of undergraduates who obtain teaching
  certification (educational measurement)
- Increase the competency of program graduates for conducting research and developing instructional materials (meteorology)
- Increase faculty research productivity in basic and applied
  psychology (psychology)
- Increase the marketability of master's program graduates
  by preparing them for available employment options,
  particularly in the medical, geriatric, and private rehabilitation sectors (rehabilitation services)
- Increase program recognition and attractiveness (move-
  ment science)

ESTABLISHING OUTCOME CRITERIA

After the outcome objectives are written, the criteria for evaluating performance on those objectives must be identified. If, for example, your program objective was to increase the number of students, criteria such as student head count, number of full-time equivalent students, number of student credit hours generated per academic year, or number of program graduates per year could be employed.

For some objectives, criteria are more difficult to identify than others. For student level of performance, for example, it would be necessary to develop criteria dealing with such complex areas as quality of doctoral dissertations, performance on examinations, or quality of jobs obtained. Because of the omnipresent phenomenon of grade inflation, it would be unwise to use grade point average as the criterion of student performance.

Criteria for assessing faculty productivity, such as number of journal publications, have already been discussed. For the assessment of program productivity, the results for individual faculty members within the same program can be accumulated.

In addition to specifying the criterion for each desired outcome, the program members must also indicate the desired level of performance on each. In other words, the outcome of increased graduate enrollment as measured against the criterion of number of graduate student credit hours generated must have a desired level of attainment or a desirable degree of gain or improvement. A good rule of thumb for goal setting is to shoot for a 10 percent increase on the criterion measures. This level of improvement is usually both challenging and attainable.

Some examples of outcome criteria are listed below:

- Research productivity of at least one refereed publication per faculty member per year
- Instructional efficiency of 25 students per undergraduate course
- Program quality reflected in a favorable review by campuswide program evaluation committee
- Student enrollment of at least 37 majors in two years

- Research visibility reflected by at least one state or national presentation per faculty member next year
- External R&D funds obtained by program faculty to be increased by 10 percent within two years

DETERMINING CURRENT OUTCOME STATUS

The third step is to determine your current status on outcome objectives. This represents the preaudit activity called for in the model. It serves the purpose of providing a benchmark against which improvement can be measured. It uses the same criteria established in the preceding step but provides an entry or starting level based on the current outcome status. In the case of enrollment, it would be the current number of full-time equivalent students. For faculty research productivity, it could be the number of refereed journal publications for the preceding year.

IDENTIFYING NEEDED REQUIREMENTS

You want to increase enrollments from level A, their current level, to level B, a 10 percent increase. What will you need to accomplish this? That is, name the requirements needed for meeting your objective. Do you need more faculty, more staff, more budget, new programs, more space? Perhaps you do not need anything in addition to what you already have.

Since the planning process is a mechanism for sharing information about needs and allocating available resources, it is important that the needed requirements for each objective be carefully and conservatively established. A requirements list would probably include the following:

- Faculty positions
- Graduate assistantships
- Clerical and support positions
- Hourly personnel
- Travel money
- Other expense money (e.g., for supplies, duplicating)

- Facilities
- Equipment

CONSTRUCTING AN ATTAINMENT PLAN

Now you know what you want to accomplish, how far you have to go, and what you need to get there. The next step is to draw up or build a plan or set of steps aimed at attaining your objective. A plan is like a road map that tells you how to get from point A to point B. It is a step-by-step sequence of actions that you judge to be necessary and sufficient to reach your goal.

Below are some examples of activities contained in various plans:

- Develop and distribute program brochures to a national audience.
- Require faculty to submit descriptions of proposed and on-going research on a yearly basis.
- Redesign the science laboratory to bring it up to date.
- Require all mathematics majors to take at least two courses on computer programming.
- Meet with history and social science faculty to identify skills courses in those areas.
- Develop a system for identifying potential doctoral students; contact the identified prospects and track those that respond.
- Identify faculty who are willing to discuss various design and analysis topics with individuals or groups of faculty or students.

DISSEMINATING PLANNING INFORMATION

It is not possible for an institution of higher education to carry out all of its plans as designed because of the combined requirements of these plans. In a college with 20 different academic programs, each of which has developed five plans that call for two new faculty positions, the net number of new positions required to carry out all the plans would be a minimum of 40. If the college has five vacant positions to allocate, it could only choose a small subset of plans to support. In order to involve all faculty in the difficult decisions of choice, it is necessary for each program to see and share the plans of all other programs.

In order to accomplish the necessary dissemination process, each plan should be edited to fill no more than one side of a single page. Each plan should consist of a statement of a single objective along with its criteria, current status, additional requirements, and plan to achieve. Figures 5.1 to 5.6 show six samples.

Planning worksheets such as these should be printed and distributed to all members of the faculty so that each can be made aware of the goals and expectations of all of the programs in the college. In the case study, this was done with a volume of more than 100 worksheets.

Figure 5.1
Sample Plan Number 1

PROGRAM:	Economics
DEPARTMENT:	Social Sciences
OBJECTIVE:	Increase graduate program recognition
CRITERIA:	-2 national meetings on program annually per faculty -maintain 1 refereed publication annually per faculty
CURRENT STATUS:	-Average: 1 national meeting on program per faculty -Average: 1 refereed publication per year
ADDITIONAL REQUIREMENTS:	-Add one faculty line -Get doctoral directive status for one more faculty member -Fund 60 clock hours weekly for graduate student research assistance -Fund 40 clock hours weekly for graduate student teaching assistance -Add four new doctoral students annually from a national pool of applicants
PLAN FOR ACHIEVEING:	Develop and distribute program brochure to national audience. Seek new avenues for involvement in national organizations and publication (Eg: journal reviews).
COLLEGE STRATEGY:	Professional Leadership/Journal Publications

Figure 5.2
Sample Plan Number 2

PROGRAM: Elementary Education

DEPARTMENT: Childhood Education

OBJECTIVE: To improve the quality of the Specialist and
                 Doctoral programs by enlarging the core of
                 courses for graduate students and by promoting
                 more collaborative research between faculty and
                 students.

CRITERIA: This objective will be evaluated by a favorable
                 review by the Graduate Policy Committee (G.P.C.)
                 on their 1988 review of our doctoral programs.
                 Both of these objectives along with more faculty
                 research were critisims from the last G.P.C.
                 review. These objectives will eliminate that
                 area of concern.

CURRENT   Currently students are required to take two
STATUS: research courses, and a third in prospectus
                 preparation is strongly recommended. The rest
                 of a doctoral student's program is guided by the
                 student's previous background and professional
                 goals and needs. There is no extended set of
                 courses which comprise a core nor are students
                 required to do research with particular faculty
                 prior to the dissertation.

ADDITIONAL   Sufficient OPS funds to assign doctoral
REQUIREMENTS: students to faculty for collaborative research
                 efforts.

PLAN FOR   -Meeting will begin in Fall 1985 to plan and
ACHIEVING: implement a core doctoral program in Elementary
                 Education.
                 -Doctoral students will be required to develop
                 two collaborative projects with elementary
                 education faculty before they begin their
                 prospectus.
                 -Students will be required to (a) take
                 supervised research hours and (b) the
                 department, through OPS funds, will support
                 graduate students for 10 hours a week in
                 research projects.
                 -Faculty will be required to submit proposed and
                 on-going research on a yearly basis. This will
                 allow students to see an overview of research
                 and to select more carefully.

COLLEGE   Improved Standards
STRATEGY:

Figure 5.3
Sample Plan Number 3

PROGRAM:	Management
DEPARTMENT:	Business Administration
OBJECTIVE:	To strengthen current linkages and expand collaboration with corporations, management development networks, business agencies and other professional organizations in providing service to improve management and organization development in the business sector.
CRITERIA:	Each faculty member will provide direct assistance as: (1) technical assistance; (2) trainer or training developer; (3) policy or advisory board member; (4) program/process evaluator; (5) O.D. consultant; (6) research/development.
CURRENT STATUS:	Only occasional technical assistance to businesses; most training based at university site; focus on delivery of traditional courses or standard noncompentency-based workshops (summer); three faculty serve on business/advisory teams; few faculty serve on evaluation teams; generally perform no evaluative or on-site activities; two faculty provide occasional O.D. consulting; minimal faculty involvement in R&D; faculty interest in above is on the increase.
ADDITIONAL REQUIREMENTS:	Resources for faculty travel/per diem to deliver on-site training and technical assistance, to work with business and agency personnel in planning for capacity building, and to receive faculty development in program delivery; half-time faculty to coordinate service effort.
PLAN FOR ACHIEVING:	Continue Management Development Council (MDC) and Management Development Network (MDN) work; develop individual faculty - business contacts for identifying training/technical assistance needs; develop a Tri-University Management Center advisory board for consulting work; engage all faculty in their own development; organize training - development teams.
COLLEGE STRATEGY:	Field Service

Figure 5.4
Sample Plan Number 4

PROGRAM: Counseling Psychology

DEPARTMENT: Psychology

OBJECTIVE: To raise the general intellectual and
                    achievement level required for admission to the
                    Doctoral Counseling Psychology Program.

CRITERIA: -Graduate Record Examination Scores: 1150 total
                    -Undergraduate Grade Point Average 3.3
                    -Graduate G.P.A. 3.5
                    -Demonstrated research competence

CURRENT   -GRE Scores: 1000
STATUS: -Undergraduate G.P.A.: 3.1*

ADDITIONAL   -Larger applicant pool
REQUIREMENTS: -Stronger "scientific" orientation to program
                    -More rigorous and extensive recruiting effort
                    -Funds to support more rigorous recruiting
                    effort
                    -Current applicant pool of approximately 60
                    should be increased to 90
                    -Current scientist-practitioner balance of 30%
                    to 70% should be shifted to 50% to 50%
                    -Recruiting effort should be increased by 25%

PLAN FOR   -Set new minimum GRE and GPA levels for
ACHIEVING: admission to the doctoral program
                    -Advertise existence of program in psychological
                    journals and association newsletter
                    -Increase publication of faculty in psychological
                    journals and attendance/presentation at
                    psychological meetings
                    -Expand admission criteria to include
                    younger/less experienced applicants for a
                    MS/Ph.D. combined degree

COLLEGE   Selective Admissions
STRAGEY:

---

*Current plan for admission targets more of a "practitioner"
applicant; therefore, this new plan of action is very different
from what currently takes place.

Figure 5.5
Sample Plan Number 5

PROGRAM: Instructional Systems

DEPARTMENT: Educational Research, Development and Foundations

OBJECTIVE: To build closer liaison with industry through internships and other activities.

CRITERIA: A closer relationship with industry will be indicated by provision of more internship opportunities for students, financial support for the program, and participation by industry in our sponsored activities.

CURRENT STATUS: Relationships have been established with several companies and, through them, internships offered. Many of the faculty participated in a seminar on instructional design done for a major corporation. However, there has been no direct financial support for the program as a result of these activities, nor has the program sponsored any activities that would attract industrial interest.

ADDITIONAL REQUIREMENTS: Faculty, in general, do not see the activities particularly appealing or academically rewarding. If left simply to the faculty to accomplish, there is some probability it will not be accomplished because of the large number of management-coordination tasks. Therefore, it is proposed that a program manager be hired for one year to coordinate the activities associated with this and several other projects. The program manager will bring in faculty at those points at which their contributions are most needed.

PLAN FOR ACHIEVING: The faculty will work as a committee of the whole to identify: 1) exactly what it is that we want to get from and provide to industry, and 2) a list of companies with which faculty have had recent relationships. Based on this information, calls will be placed to the representatives and trips planned when appropriate. We will also attempt to work with our own graduates who are employed in industry, and to meet with industry representatives at national meetings in order to save costs associated with travel.

COLLEGE STRATEGY: Speculative Initiative

70

Figure 5.6
Sample Plan Number 6

PROGRAM:	Graduate Program
DEPARTMENT:	Public Administration
OBJECTIVE:	Establish a week-end program for the adult clientele of the PA Program who can not attend classes during the regular weekdays or nights.
CRITERIA:	Enrollment of 15 or more students in each cycle, beginning Fall 1985 (Fall 1986 next, then no new students for a year while cycle 1 students try to become doctoral candidates and begin work on their proposals.
CURRENT STATUS:	A program has been approved by the PA faculty, agreed to by the Department Chairman and sent to the Dean; authorization for and approval of arrangements to proceed are awaited.
ADDITIONAL REQUIREMENTS:	(1) All three PA sub-field must be staffed with full-time faculty. (2) The PA building first floor must be opened and heated or air conditioned on the weekends on which classes are to be held. (3) Policies must be made about the percent of FTE assignment allowable for teaching on the weekend and the days of week which faculty may be absent when they teach on the weekend. (4) No future commitments should be made to offer doctoral programs off-campus if this program is approved for implementation, UNLESS one more full time position is authorized for a person who is qualified to teach, do and direct research, counsel off-campus students on site, and assist the Department Head in coordinating all non-traditional program(s).
PLAN FOR ACHIEVING:	(1) Program plan fully developed and an informal needs assessment conducted which justifies the operation of this kind of program. The program plan on file with the Dean needs to be approved as soon as possible. (2) Discontinue current negotiations for a new cycle of the off-campus PA Program or receive another position to replace the coordinator of the off-campus program who has changed positions. (3) If a new position is made available, recruit a faculty member who is expert in the non-traditional delivery of instruction.
COLLEGE STRATEGY:	Development Project

71

COLLEGE STRATEGIES

Because of the great number of program objectives and concomitant resource requirements relative to available funds, it is
useful to think of and formulate overarching strategies that might
be used to accomplish combinations of objectives at the same time.
These strategies would enable a variety of programs with similar
objectives to combine their efforts in meeting these objectives,
thereby cutting down on the costs.

For example, many programs might identify "targeted recruitment of students" as a major step in their plan to increase student
enrollment. If the college were to assign resources to the targeted
recruitment strategy by paying for the development and mailing
of attractive program brochures, it would facilitate the recruitment
process for all programs that participated. In addition, a travel
grant program for subsidizing faculty travel to professional meetings with student recruitment as part of their task would aid in
efforts to recruit students.

A detailed listing of 12 college strategies distributed across input,
process, and output categories, with examples of programmatic
efforts within each strategy, appears in Table 5.1.

A useful task within the planning process is to classify all planning objectives into one of the 12 college strategies in order to
identify those that can be achieved through the simultaneous use
of resources. This can be accomplished using the form shown in
Figure 5.7. In other words, all recruitment objectives would be
classified together, all objectives calling for developmental efforts,
all objectives calling for trained professionals, and so on. This
classification process can make the choices for resource allocation
clearer because it enables decision makers to determine how many
plans can be implemented at the same time through a single
allocation.

CHOOSING AMONG STRATEGIES

It is more efficient to try to choose among strategies, since there
are only 12, than to try, initially, to choose among 100 or so
objectives. Moreover, choosing among strategies takes some of

Table 5.1
College Strategies to Accomplish College Missions

I. INPUT (Maximize resources and their use)

    A. Targeted Student Recruitment (travel grants, brochure development, community college campus visitations)

    B. Selective Student Admissions (computerized recordkeeping of applications)

    C. Faculty Planning (development of objectives and plans, planning retreats)

    D. Selective Initiatives (Proposals for Action, subsidy of conferences)

II. PROCESS (Improve existing tasks; respond to new needs)

    A. Organizational Adjustments (relocation of programs in departments, restructuring of research center)

    B. Improved Standards (Research Advisory Committee to review dissertation proposals, requirement for GRE's)

    C. Research Proposals (preparing proposals for State and Federal grants)

    D. Development Projects (science needs assessment, new teacher education programs being developed)

III. OUTPUT (Shared results)

    A. Trained Professionals (certificate program in Human Resource Development, accreditation of Counseling Psychology program)

    B. Journal Publications (statistical consultation center, word processing services)

    C. Professional Leadership (faculty travel grants, hosting of regional meetings)

    D. Field Service (management development center, teacher education center)

Figure 5.7
A Form for Classifying Program Objectives by Collegewide Strategy

Strategy:	INPUT — Maximize Resources & Use				PROCESS — Improve Existing Tasks / Respond To New Needs				OUTPUT — Share Results			
Program:	Targeted Recruiting	Selective Admissions	Faculty Planning	Speculative Initiatives	Organizational Adjustments	Improved Standards	Development Projects	Research Proposals	Trained Professionals	Journals Publications	Professional Leadership	Field Service
Early/Child												
Elem. Educ.												
Reading												
Sci. Educ.												
Spec. Educ.												
Eng. Educ.												
Math. Educ.												
Lang. Educ.												
Soc. Studies												
Adult Educ.												
Educ. Admin.												
Voc. Educ.												
Higher Educ.												
Educ. Found												
Resch. & Eval.												
Inst. Sys.												
Counseling												
Health												
Leisure												
Rehab.												
Phy. Ed.												
Movement Sc.												

the focus off programs and places it on the college as a total organization. This happens because the strategy is a college-level unit with its target being college-level outcomes, while the objective is a program-level unit with its target being program-level outcomes. In choosing among programs' specific outcomes, loyalty to one's own program unit can be a biasing factor. This should be minimized in choosing among college-specific strategies.

A useful procedure for choosing among strategies is one called paired comparison. In paired comparison, each alternative is compared directly to every other alternative in order to produce an order of preference. A program for use in a personal computer for paired comparison is available through Decision Support Software, Inc. The program is called EXPERT CHOICE and will be used to illustrate the choice process. It is based on the work of Saaty (1977, 1980) on the analytic hierarchy process.

The first set of comparisons involves the four input strategies in order to determine which is the most important in terms of maximizing resources through efficient use of funds. Each of the four strategies—targeted recruiting, selective admissions, faculty planning, and speculative initiatives—is compared to each of the others, and a judge indicates the more important member of each pair and its relative degree of greater importance (extreme, very strong, strong, moderate). The choices may also be judged to be equally important.

The next result is that each choice ends up with an importance score between zero and one, with the higher score reflecting greater judged importance. Each judge generates his or her own set of importance scores for each strategy relative to the others.

The process is then repeated in terms of importance for improving existing tasks and responding to new needs (i.e., process). The strategies compared here are organizational adjustments, improving standards, developmental projects, and research proposals. The final cycle of comparisons is done in terms of gaining recognition through shared results (output) and involves the production of trained professionals, journal publications, professional leadership, and field services.

This process was carried out by three deans and eight department heads in the same college. The deans placed heavy emphasis on speculative initiatives and developmental projects in the input and process areas since they had committed themselves to innovation at the faculty level as the mechanism for moving the college forward. The department heads' choices reflected on the relative strengths and weaknesses of each department and which strategy would enhance one's own department to the greatest degree. Hence, the head of a department with a significant number of researchers endorsed all strategies that favored research, while the head of a department with a heavy training responsibility favored strategies oriented toward training. The advantage of the quantitative approach provided by the computer is that it makes clear what choices each person favors since it requires that choices be made and weighted.

It must be noted that the strategies identified will be specific to the organization in question and the mission of that organization. The strategies identified for consideration in a liberal arts college may be quite different from those of an engineering school, for example. Also, the organizational level of respondents can vary all the way from the leader to each and every one of the members, and decisions can be analyzed and compared across and among any and all levels and units.

CHOOSING AMONG OBJECTIVES

The final step in the planning process is choosing those objectives you wish to attain and allocating organizational resources accordingly. This is unavoidably a "judgment call," but it can be based, at least in part, on the relative importance of the various college strategies. It can also be based on the judgments of individual faculty, program coordinators, department heads, and administrators.

In order to make judgments and allocations regarding objectives and resources, each judge must have the following information:

- A list of each program's top three objectives along with a statement of the requirements for meeting each objective and a plan for each
- Information about the latest productivity of each program in terms of instruction, research, and service

- Information about the current number of faculty in each program and imminent retirements
- Classification of each objective in terms of college strategy
- Ratings of the various college strategies by different level groups within the college
- A list of resources that are currently available for allocation

It is recommended that the process of judging objectives and recommending resource allocations be done at a half-day or full-day session called a planning retreat. Participants could be all faculty members, all program coordinators, all department heads, all deans and deans' staff, or any combination of these. All participants should have all of the necessary information in advance so that they can study it and become familiar with it.

If the number of participants is large, they should be assigned to small groups so that group membership cuts across program areas. Each group should have a predesignated group leader and all group leaders should go through a briefing and debriefing. Each group should be asked to allocate all of the available resources by assigning resources to objectives. Resources may be given in units of faculty lines, staff support lines, graduate assistantships, hourly wages, or expense dollars.

We will return to the matter of resource allocation and distribution among programs in Chapter 7, where we will look at a basis for accomplishing this using data contained within the management information system combined with the outcome management model. But, first, our discussion of planning will continue with the presentation of additional procedures.

6

The Role of Faculty Plans

This chapter will focus on the plan as the representation of intended behavior and show how the planning process may be applied to individual faculty members in an effort to enhance both their performance and that of the organization. Two kinds of plans will be described. The first is called the academic assignment plan and sets forth the faculty members' intended instructional, research, and service activity. The second kind of plan is called a proposal for action (the terms "plan" and "proposal" are used interchangeably) and represents a special kind of plan that is made in order to attempt to receive special support in an effort to attain objectives of particular value to the organization.

The framework for viewing and understanding both of these kinds of plans is shown in Figure 6.1.

ACADEMIC ASSIGNMENT PLANS

In order to attempt to achieve both individual and organizational objectives, plans must be drawn up by each faculty member in close consultation with department heads and central administra-

Figure 6.1
Framework for Viewing Plans Within the Outcome Management
Context

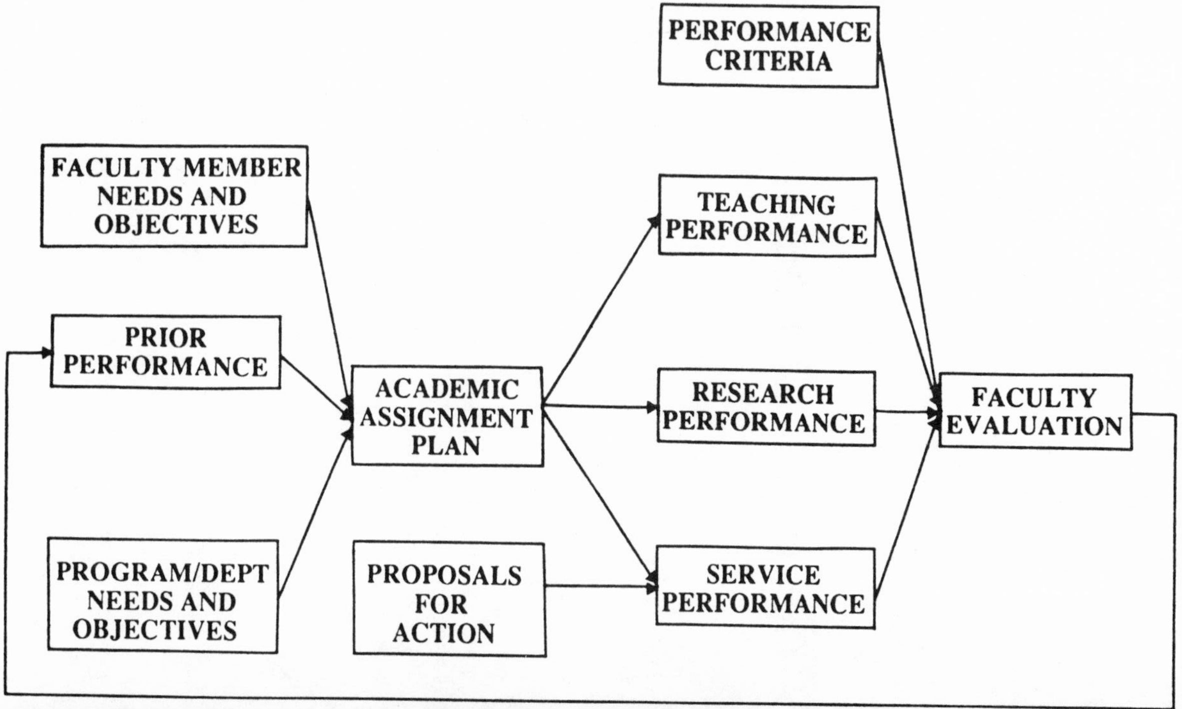

tion. The initiative or initial specification must come from the appropriate administrator as regards to the division of a faculty member's assignment among instruction, research, and service, and the specific instructional and advisement responsibilities that the faculty member will be expected to carry out. We will focus here on the aspects of the plan that are usually left to the faculty member's own initiative, that is, the research and service activities to be undertaken. It is most common for these latter aspects not to be spelled out, but for all to assume that they will take place. In other words, while a plan will be drawn up to describe the instructional and advisement activities of the faculty member, no plan is usually drawn up to describe his or her research and service activities. Time is usually allotted to both research and service activities, but no advance plans are formulated.

One of the basic assumptions of outcome management is that the likelihood of attaining an objective is increased if a plan is first drawn up. The value of the plan is both motivational and directional. It is motivational because it helps you muster the energy to act. It is directional because it tells you how to act. It also provides you with something against which to compare the results of your action.

Think of classes you have sat through where the teacher had no apparent plan. Didn't they seem pointless and purposeless? Weren't you constantly waiting for the point to be made? The same applies to individual research and service. Without a plan, neither may ever happen.

To overcome the very real possibility of inaction, each faculty member is asked to submit, prior to the start of the school year, a Research Assignment Plan and a Service Assignment Plan. Each follows the same format and, for each intended research and service project or activity, requires a single page listing the following:

- Title

- Objective(s)

- Plan of action and timeline (including completion date)

- Intended product(s)

Samples of each type of plan appear in Figures 6.2 and 6.3.

At the end of the school year, each faculty member is asked to submit a list of accomplishments from which individual, program,

Figure 6.2
A Sample Research Assignment Plan

```
Title:    An  Investigation  of the Effectiveness  of  a  Study
          Skills  Program on the Academic Performance of Fourth
          Grade Students.

Objective(s):        1)  To prepare a two-week study skills unit.

                     2)  To discover whether fourth graders who
                         are  taught the two-week study  skills
                         unit  develop better study skills than
                         those who are not taught the unit.

                     3)  To discover whether fourth graders who
                         are taught the unit earn higher grades
                         than  those  who are  not  taught  the
                         unit.

Plan of Activities: 1)  Search    the    literature    to   find
                         available  study skills  instructional
                         materials  and  adapt  them  for  this
                         study (September 1).

                     2)  Make  arrangements with a local school
                         to teach the unit (October 1).

                     3)  Find  or  develop  a  suitable   study
                         skills test (September 1).

                     4)  Carry  out  the instruction  and  data
                         collection (January 1).

                     5)  Analyze the data (March 1)

                     6)  Write the report (June 1)

Intended Product(s):1)  Final report

                     2)  Journal article
```

Figure 6.3
A Sample Service Assignment Plan

Title: A   workshop   on   the   use   of   micro-computers   for
            diagnosis of reading difficulties.

Objective(s):   1)   To   identify   the   rate   of   context   to
                          content errors.

                     2)   To   master   the operation of the   READ
                          software   package   for a   90%   correct
                          diagnosis   of   a   demonstration   video
                          tape.

Plan: Three workshops are to be held as   in-
                          service sessions for special education
                          teachers at three different elementary
                          schools.   One   faculty member and   two
                          graduate   assistants will conduct   the
                          workshops   and   present   follow-up
                          meetings   to   validate   diagnosis   on
                          actual cases.

End Product: The   READ program should be a part   of
                          the   County   School   System   special
                          education diagnostic procedures by the
                          Fall of 1986.

---

and college productivity measures are determined. Within this list
of accomplishments, each faculty member would be expected to
list the outcomes or products that resulted from each Research
Assignment Plan and each Service Assignment Plan.

There are two additional values associated with the use of assignment plans. The first is that the extent to which such plans are
carried out becomes a meaningful basis for the annual evaluation
of each faculty member. The second value is that the actual occurrence of planned activities can form the basis for subsequent
divisions of a faculty member's time. Those faculty members who
do not carry out proposed research and service plans would not
be given the same percentage of time assignment to devote to
research and service the following year. One's own time is a val-
uable resource, and research and service time can and should be
awarded on the basis of prior performance.

PROPOSALS FOR ACTION

It has been strongly argued that change is most likely to occur if it proceeds from the bottom up rather than from the top down. To this end, it is important not only to give faculty members an opportunity to generate plans for achieving their objectives but to provide them with financial resources to implement their plans.

In their well-known book, *In Search of Excellence*, Peters and Waterman identify local or employee-level initiative as a major source of product improvement. They coin the name *skunk works* to identify those grass-roots or nonbureaucratized efforts at change. In higher education, as in commercial industry, meaningful and lasting change requires the establishment of or support for such skunk works. The administrator must play the role of *champion*, to use another Peters and Waterman term, in supporting faculty efforts aimed toward productivity.

In order to select among available options provided by faculty, there must be some overall organizational scheme that allows plans to be evaluated relative to organizational goals. The collegewide strategies described in the previous chapter can serve this purpose well. As useful as the strategies can be for choosing among objectives, they can be equally useful in choosing between plans.

The mechanism chosen for accomplishing the purpose of supporting faculty initiatives in the college of education case study was a program called proposals for action. This was an in-house program for distributing funds to faculty on the basis of proposals submitted. Faculty members were invited to submit proposals that fit one of the three categories described below:

- Efficient resource utilization, including better ways to use funds to recruit more and better students, to improve admissions procedures, to increase use of and participation in planning, and to initiate new projects on a pilot basis.

- Responsiveness to needs, covering efforts to adjust the organization, to improve standards, to develop new programs, and to propose new research.

- Increased visibility or recognition, including placement of graduates, research projects leading to quality publications, leadership in state, regional, and national associations, and service to school districts and public agencies.

Faculty members received the call for proposals at the end of the academic year or early in the summer and proposals were due in three weeks after the start of classes in the fall. Three weeks later awards were announced and funding began. All proposals had to have as senior author a full-time faculty member whose line was budgeted within the college. A maximum of $25,000 was allocated for the entire proposal program with no proposal receiving more than $2,500. A research advisory committee made up of one faculty member from each department reviewed all proposals and made recommendations to the administration of which to support.

Each proposal had a cover sheet, including a 50-word abstract, and a two-page, single-spaced narrative. The narrative included a description of rationale and need, plan of action and timeline, and statement of financial and nonfinancial resources needed. In addition, each proposal had to indicate which of one or more of the three categories of college goals (as listed above) it was addressed to and what its intended impact was on this goal or goals.

Funding was for a one-year period, but continuation funding for a second year could be applied for. All grant recipients were required to submit a progress report or final report at the end of the year's funding period. The timeline for the process is shown below.

In evaluating proposals for action as a strategy for change, it is instructive to examine the results. In the first year of the program, 70 proposals were submitted by a faculty of about 140. In the second year that number was reduced to about 50, primarily because of the expectation for continuation funding. As faculty would come forward seeking funds for various research and development initiatives, they were encouraged to plan to submit a proposal for action at the next opportunity. In other words, this program became an alternative to ad hoc funding.

It is instructive to examine a sampling of some of the 14 projects funded in the second year, the majority of which were continuations of first-year funded projects. Seven of them are described below.

The Construction of a Program in Human Resource Development. This project spanned two years and resulted in the offering of a 15-hour Certificate Program in Human Resource Development (HRD) aimed primarily at middle managers in state agencies. The program was built around existing courses and could be used toward a master's degree with an emphasis on HRD. The new program combined two program areas in need of student enrollments, adult education and research and evaluation, and drew 20 new students to its first offering.

Assessing Regional Needs in Secondary-Level Science, Mathematics, and Computers. In anticipation of monies becoming available to establish a regional center in these subject areas, a series of six meetings was held throughout the region to identify local needs. A study team of faculty visited the campus of each of the six community colleges in the region to attend a meeting to which representatives from all surrounding public school districts were invited. Local participants completed a needs assessment questionnaire, the results of which were then presented and discussed, and a plan for cooperative efforts was generated.

Hosting a Regional Meeting of a National Organization. A conference ws held dealing with the social context and implication of the educational reform process at the state level. The conference drew 140 professionals from throughout the region and featured speakers of national note. It provided an important opportunity to form linkages among persons interested in the topic of educational policy formulation and established the role and contribution of the sponsoring institution.

Offering a Symposium on Motivating Black Students toward Excellence in Academic Achievement and Testing. The purpose of the symposium was to gather ideas and materials for a resource guide on the topic. The symposium drew 71 participants and yielded nine descriptions of projects that had been successful in improving the achievement of black students.

Development of a Computerized Testing Capability. This project was aimed at establishing a microcomputer-managed testing system within the college. After two years of funding, the necessary software was developed and the implementation of the operating system was imminent. It will permit students to be administered tests, individually, outside of the classroom; to receive immediate feedback; and to be retested as appropriate. The system will maintain student records for instructors, manage the pacing of students, and provide instructors with test item analysis. It will also process group-administered examinations and questionnaires. The software is user-friendly (i.e., menu driven) with 11 main menu options. It is written mostly in the C programming language. It was pilot-tested on three courses.

Personal Fitness Implementation Study. This was a study of ninth grade students across the state who participated in a mandated course in personal fitness as the high school physical education requirement. The effect of the course was determined by measuring performance, knowledge, and attitudes of students who took it on a pre and post basis. As a result of this project and the presentation of its results at a national meeting, Project FIT (Fitness Inventory Testing) was developed as a service for the state's public schools to provide evaluation of the personal fitness course on a fee basis.

A Study of the Effect of Adult Behaviors on Children's Learning from Instructional Television. During the year, research data were collected from 97 preschoolchildren who individually watched three specially edited episodes of "Sesame Street" in the presence of an adult. These data will be analyzed and a paper written for publication. Efforts were also made to obtain external funding to extend this line of research.

All 14 projects are listed and categorized by collegewide strategy in Table 6.1.

THE IMPACT OF PLANNING

Remember that the sequence of events in outcome management is to (1) set goals; (2) measure where you stand on those goals, that is, how far you need to progress to reach them; (3) develop a plan for goal attainment; and (4) measure your status in relation to the goal after the plan has been implemented, that is, test

Table 6.1
14 Proposals for Action by Collegewide Strategy

EFFICIENT USE OF RESOURCES	RESPONSIVENESS TO NEEDS	INCREASED RECOGNITION
Develop Program in Human Resources Development	Assess Regional Needs in Science, Math	Host Regional Meeting of Nat'l Organization
Recruit new students in Visual Disabilities	Offer Symposium on Motivating Black Students	Conduct & publish a study on children's learning from T.V.
Extend a computer-managed, field experience program	Improve Students' Reading & Writing	Conduct & publish a study of academic learning time
Develop computerized testing	Improve Diagnosis in Reading & Writing	Conduct & publicize a study of personal fitness
	Evaluate Effective Teaching Career	
	Develop a Career Measure for Adults in Transition	

whether or not you have made it to the goal. The whole sequence can then be repeated.

Also, recall that the primary focus of outcome management is the organization rather than the individual faculty member and so the goals are organizational goals. (In the instance of the case study, those goals were efficient resource utilization, responsiveness to needs, and increased visibility or recognition.) In order for the organization to be successful, it must maximize performance on its goals. However, organizations do not act; only the members of organizations act. Hence, the organization can meet its goals only if the faculty members contribute to such organizational goal attainment through their own individual efforts. In order for this to happen, faculty members must endorse organizational goals, build plans for their attainment, and be rewarded for helping the organization get there.

It is not necessary for a faculty member to feel coerced to expend effort on behalf of the organization when there is a correspondence between organizational goals and individual goals. For example, faculty members seek individual recognition based on their own professional contributions and these same contributions contribute to organizational recognition as well. Also, faculty members may deliver professional services in order to achieve personal financial gain but those services may also help the organization to meet its goal of responsiveness. Finally, faculty members themselves desire more and better students so that they will have someone to teach and this, simultaneously, has the potential to contribute to organizational efficiency.

One potential impact of planning is to identify actions that will further both organizational goals and the individual goal attainment of the faculty members who carry them out. Sometimes this is accomplished extrinsically, that is, by providing faculty members with additional resources or remuneration for doing something for the organization. Equally often, it is accomplished intrinsically, that is, through planned actions that increase the likelihood of attainment of both individual and organizational goals. In the case of a planning approach such as proposals for action, faculty members voluntarily build plans to help attain organizational goals (and usually individual ones as well) and are given direct financial assistance (and recognition) to carry out their plans. In the case of the assignment plans for research and service, faculty members must involuntarily account for the way they will spend assigned time with the expectation that there will be negative consequences following a failure to carry out plans as proposed.

The quality and value of planning, as well as its likely impact, will be influenced not only by the correspondence (or lack thereof) between individual and organizational goals but by what might be called the motivation behind the planning, that is, whether the planning is essentially self-motivated or motivated by imposed organizational requirements. In the case of the college of education case study, the faculty reaction to proposals for action was quite different from the reaction to assignment plans. In the case of proposals for action, as was mentioned earlier, an extremely large number of proposals was submitted without an exceptional amount of administrative urging. In the case of the assignment plans, getting the faculty to submit them was literally like pulling teeth, and many that were received were minimal in their detail or the amount of useful information they contained.

The idea behind research and service assignment planning was to increase faculty performance relative to the amount of time allocated for the purposes of pursuing research and service activities. In the college of education case study, the practice has not been in effect long enough to determine whether the formulation of such plans constituted an exercise in plan building and little else. The key to the impact of the practice, however, may be in the consequences that are attached to it. At the end of each academic year, each faculty member is required to submit reports of progress relative to both research and service assignment plans.

For purposes of convenience and to minimize the intrusiveness of the management process, a format should be developed to enable faculty members to combine their progress reports and the reports they submit in application for annual merit and discretionary raises (see Chapter 8) into a single document that can serve both purposes: accountability and reward. Combining these two functions into a single report may reduce some of the reluctance and discomfort on the part of faculty to accept the fact that they are expected to convert assignments of time into productive outcomes.

For many faculty members, the act of planning projects to fill allocated time may be a sufficient inducement to carry out those plans. Particularly for those who desire to accomplish research and service activities, the plan may provide both direction and impetus so that the result is productive. For those who comply with the letter of the planning requirement but not the spirit, there must be consequences or the entire planning process will become a sham. Those consequences must be reflected in two ways: on the annual performance evaluation for that year, and in the assignment of time for research and service for the succeeding year.

An annual evaluation of the performance of individual faculty members is a common practice. This evaluation of teaching, research, and service for the year ending is usually completed by department heads, who are usually also responsible for making faculty time assignments for the coming year. It is at this point and at this level that research and service assignment plans and annual progress reports must be examined side by side in order to determine their correspondence or lack thereof. Where progress has been made, satisfactory evaluations should be given and research and service assignments for the coming year maintained insofar as possible. Where progress is nil, department heads' evaluations must reflect and document official concern or unsatisfactory rating, and assignments for the following year should be adjusted accordingly. The arrangement is illustrated in Figure 6.4.

We will return to the matter of productivity and its impact on individual outcomes in Chapter 8.

Figure 6.4
Planning Outcomes and Their Consequences

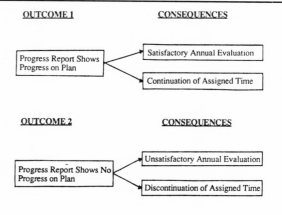

7

Decisions about Academic Programs

We now turn to the decision-making process within the context of the outcome management model. Goals have been set, outcome measures of goal attainment have been developed and applied within a management information system, and plans for goal attainment have been developed and applied at both the individual and program levels. Decisions must now be made about the allocation of resources, first to academic programs and then to individual faculty members. This chapter is devoted to allocations at the program level; the next chapter, to allocations at the individual level.

The allocation of resources at the program level must be consistent with measured program productivity within the outcome management framework. In other words, the basis for allocating resources to programs will be the degree of productivity manifested by the program. The result of such allocations will be not only to change the size of program—that is, adding positions to make programs larger or subtracting positions (often through retirements) to make them smaller—but also to change the organizational chart—that is, larger programs swallowing smaller ones or smaller programs merging to form larger ones.

In other management systems, organizational chart decisions are

made on a political basis (i.e., who wants them); in outcome management, they are made (as you shall see) on the basis of management information, planning, and productivity. Moreover, even
within outcome management, it is critical to regard the chart as a
conclusion about relationships (that is, the result of outcomes) and
not to view it as a mechanism for controlling a system. An analogy
from meteorology makes the point. It would be absurd to think
that changes in the humidity gauge would change either the temperature or the dew point. The gauge will change only when relationships between temperature and dew point change. Yet it is
not uncommon for college committees on organizational change
to begin their deliberations by asking, What changes do we need
to make in our organizational chart in order to improve
productivity?

The purpose of this chapter is to answer this question in reverse,
that is, not by starting with an organizational chart but by starting
with the data on instructional productivity. These data include both
classroom teaching assignments, undergraduate and graduate, and
advising responsibilities for graduate students. We will conclude
this chapter by recommending modifications in the organizational
chart, but only after considerable discussion about the process of
transforming students into degree holders and other input to outcome relationships. The discussion about academic programs focuses on faculty members as the major source for accomplishing
the transformation and primarily utilizes instructional productivity
data.

THE PRODUCTIVITY VARIABLES

We will continue to use our model of input, process, and implementation and outcome variables for the faculty role as either
teacher, adviser, researcher, or provider of services. Figure 7.1
displays those characteristics that are measurable for each variable.

Faculty Roles

The columns in Figure 7.1 represent the various tasks faculty
members are assigned in order to meet their academic responsibilities. The role of classroom teacher typically occupies more than

Figure 7.1
Measures of Faculty Productivity for Roles of Teacher, Major Professor, Research Scholar, and Service Provider

	Classroom Teacher	Major Professor	Research Scholar	Service Provider
INPUT	Students Taught: Course Load x No. of Students Enrolled	Majors Advised Variable Credits for Individuals	Time Assigned	Time Assigned
PROCES	Number of Course Credits per Program	Number of Variable Credits per Program	Competence	Reputation
OUTCOME	Number of Student Credit Hours	Number of Degrees Awarded	Articles Published, Papers Presented, and Reports Written	Consultations

half of the faculty member's time, with many considerations going into the decision of how much time should be allowed for particular courses.

The variables here have to do with (1) the subject matter itself (a course in music may involve an hour for one student and one teacher, while a lecture on insurance law might involve several hundred students and one teacher); (2) the amount of time required to prepare for a class (a lecture/demonstration in chemistry may require a great deal of preparation each time the demonstration is given, while the insurance law lecture might require only minor modifications in the text of the lecture itself); and (3) the amount of time students require for individual attention (a course in mathematics that requires daily homework may take considerably more instructor's time outside the classroom than a course in European history where students are examined only several times in the term).

These most significant differences about the relationship between a faculty member's role and the time assigned to it are best determined at the lowest possible administrative level. The department chair or program leader is the best administrator to evaluate the relationship between courses and time required to teach them.

Once the classroom teaching portion of the faculty load has been assigned, the next consideration is the role of the faculty member as major professor or adviser for students. Again, the exact amount of time required to perform this role varies, depending on (1) the level of the degree sought (undergraduate students may need some guidance regarding procedures, requirements, and occasionally career planning, while doctoral students involved in dissertations may require weekly discussions relating to complex subject matter issues); (2) the complexity of the curriculum (in some professional programs like engineering and nursing, students have few options in the elective courses they can take, while in other disciplines such as English or history the number of course electives gives them many more choices and a greater need for advice from a senior faculty member); and (3) whether or not the curriculum is in an academic discipline or a professional school (English majors usually require little career guidance, while students in nursing need to be introduced to the conventions of the profession through internships and other opportunities for personal guidance).

In our particular case study of the college of education, the assignment of advising responsibilities is usually included as a part of the overall instructional responsibility and, by and large, is determined through negotiation between the faculty member and the department head. Advising master's degree students, for example, is so routine in some programs that one faculty member can advise several dozen students and carry a normal teaching load in addition.

The research and service responsibilities are discussed at length elsewhere in this book, but as we considered the whole faculty load, it seemed that these responsibilities represented the noninstructional part of the assignment. Faculty members were given their classroom assignments several months in advice; the assignments of advisees was relatively fixed from term to term and then what time remained was allocated to the research and service portion of their assignments.

Input

The rows in Figure 7.1 represent the various levels of input, process, and outcome. There are really only two inputs: numbers of students who need to be turned into holders of degrees, and time spent by faculty members that needs to be turned into some form of publication. Students are admitted to particular programs, become majors in those programs, and require commitments by faculty members to serve as advisers. Students need to be taught in formal courses, but not necessarily in the department in which they enroll as a major. As we stated above, the remaining research and service time is usually a residual from the instructional assignments and provides the input for faculty members' publications.

Process

It is in the area of administrative process or planning that we have focused some of our attention in this book. First of all, we need to know the number of fixed credit courses in each program and we need to know the relationship between the number of courses in the catalogue and the number of courses actually taught. Some faculty members believe that program growth and development is accomplished by merely increasing the number of courses offered without sufficient regard for student demand. It is a disservice to students, bordering on the unethical, to advertise a curriculum by listing courses in the catalogue when in fact the courses are seldom if ever offered. University rules that say that "any course which is not offered at least once during a given two-year period needs to be rejustified" is one mechanism for keeping the curriculum at a realistic level. Other administrative devices can be employed, but responsible management will take upon itself the obligation to monitor the curriculum to be sure that it is an active and productive one.

The variable credit courses, which usually involve more independent work with individual students, are best used when clear instructional objectives are being met and most often misused when courses that do not have sufficient enrollment are taught, with two or three students under some variable credit designation such as directed independent study.

The processing of research and service is perhaps the most difficult area of all. It would be unthinkable to direct the research activities of any faculty member or to suggest what or how a particular idea ought or ought not be pursued. Some general guidelines do help to avoid serious complications with this portion of the assignment. For example, it is important to establish the concept that faculty members are to maintain their competence on their own time. At first this seems difficult for faculty members to accept but, from a management point of view, the institution is paying the faculty member for a particular level of competence and the salary is based on that competence. One does not expect to be charged for the time it takes a plumber or a brain surgeon to become proficient enough to fulfill the services of a contract.

Time spent reading professionals journals or mastering current procedures should be a portion of a faculty member's own professional development and not paid for by the institution in addition to or as a part of the salary. The sabbatical leave is designed to provide some opportunity for faculty members to revitalize their professional competence once every several years. Other guidelines relating to sponsored or unsponsored projects, projects with a clear output, and projects that are considered by peers to be vital to the development of the disciplines can and should be developed.

Outcome

The last row in Figure 7.1 represents outcomes, and, for fixed instruction, number of student credit hours taught becomes the objective outcome. When enough credit hours have been accumulated at the proper level, the student becomes a degree holder. These student credit hours may be earned in the academic department where the student is a major or in other academic departments, and so the accounting for the productivity needs to be apportioned among the various departments; but the degree itself becomes an outcome of a particular department. Therefore, the number of degrees awarded becomes a measure of advising.

Finally the measure of research and service output is articles published, papers presented, reports written, and consultations. In the case study we have counted only published articles as a measure of the number of publications. However, the number of contracts and grants awarded and the number of papers presented, as well as other research and service outputs, could be used to identify the relationship between the percentage of research time assigned and the outputs that are valued by peers in order to complete the input, process, and output matrix of faculty roles.

When this system is made operational for a given term and a given program, as we shall now do, these relationships can be seen more clearly.

ANALYZING PROGRAM PRODUCTIVITY

The system for accounting for faculty activity (F.A.C.T.) and the annual assignments made by administrative units, described in Chapter 3, provide the measurements needed for a productivity analysis of each program based on the productivity of its faculty. Our case study illustrates how we used these data to identify needed changes in the organizational chart for our academic programs and evaluated the implications of possible decisions regarding the allocation of positions.

Instruction

Table 7.1 presents productivity measures for the 22 academic programs in the college of education case study arranged in de-

Table 7.1
Scores on Measures of Faculty Productivity for Roles of Teacher, Major Professor, Research Scholar, and Service Provider for Each of 22 Programs

Program	One Term — Teaching				One Term — Advising				5 Years	
	FTEF Positions INST	TOTAL	%INST	Students FTES	U.G.	M&S	Ph.D	Total	Research Articles	Service Papers
1	7.7	8	96	81	138	13	24	175	78	242
2	5.9	10	59	21		30	55	85	16	17
3	5.1	8	64	36	80	51	16	147	53	67
4	4.2	7	60	30	44	16	10	70	20	36
5	4.1	7	59	23		14	25	39	29	25
6	3.7	6	62	27		6	33	39	34	36
7	3.7		46	22		33	35	68	99	52
8	3.7	7	53	16		12	35	47	12	33
9	3.5	5	70	18	8	29	25	62	24	15
10	3.4	5	68	37		57	51	108	35	44
11	3.3	5	66	59	310	50	6	366	12	31
12	3.2	5	64	32		24	10	34	41	7
13	3.0	4	75	39	80	16		96	32	13
14	2.8	3	93	5		2	17	19	5	23
15	2.7	4	67	15		22	31	53	23	81
16	2.1	3	70	10		13	23	36	3	32
17	2.1	3	70	20	31	18	9	58	14	13
18	2.0	3	67	16	27	23	5	55	22	2
19	1.8	3	60	13	34	23	11	68	14	7
20	1.8	2	90	15	23	4	4	31	37	0
21	1.4	2	70	8	17	8		25	21	14
22	1.1	2	55	4	11	8		19	3	1

creasing order based on the number of full-time equivalent faculty members in the program. In other words, programs at the top have more faculty resources to use, while those at the bottom have fewer. The second column of Table 7.1 (labeled Total) displays the actual number of faculty members in the program, and the third column (%INST) indicates the percentage of faculty assignment to instruction and is an average of the percentage of available time assigned to instruction. The number of instructional positions (labeled INST in column 1) can be arrived at by multiplying column 2 (Total) by column 3 (%INST).

The instructional percentage (%INST) in column 3 is important because it indicates the degree to which a given program is required by a combination of student enrollment and budget to use faculty resources as opposed to using graduate assistants to accomplish the instructional mission of the program. Converted faculty positions can be used to pay for graduate assistants, who may produce more student credit hours per dollar than faculty members. Programs that utilize graduate assistants for instruction often enable faculty to have more free time for research and service activities. Administrators need to monitor this relationship between faculty and graduate assistants to be sure that high-quality instruction is being performed in the classroom and that the use of graduate assistants for instruction is consistent with the program's instructional goals and with the graduate students' own professional needs.

The next column (4) is the measure of full-time equivalent students (FTES) enrolled by program. Many measures could be used here, such as student credit hours, head count students, or weighted section credits. We selected FTES because it gives a weight to different levels of instruction and provides us with a comparable measure for different programs. For example, the number of undergraduate students in a large lecture does not add materially to a faculty member's work load, while the addition of four or five doctoral students to an advanced seminar does directly increase the demand for supervision. While the balance between the number of students and the amount of faculty time required is best established at the lowest administrative level, some weights are necessary to make realistic comparisons with other programs in the college or with similar programs at other institutions. In the

calculation of FTES, 15 undergraduate credits constitute one
FTES, while 12 graduate credits constitute one FTES.

Advisement

The advising load for a particular program needs to be examined
in terms of the balance between undergraduate and graduate advising and provides the administrator with some indication of the
ability of an academic program to support itself. It is very difficult
for exclusively graduate programs to take advantage of the flexibility available to programs that are both graduate and undergraduate in measuring faculty load assignments, particularly in the
use of graduate assistants. Graduate assistants cannot be properly
used in instruction at the graduate level, and so converting faculty
lines to graduate assistantships tends to be a counterproductive
process for graduate programs. Columns 5, 6, and 7 identify the
number of students to be advised at each of three program levels.
(Master's and specialist's program levels have been combined.)
Column 8 indicates the total number of majors in the program
across the three levels. In our analysis, we will be using only the
last column (column 8) as a measure of advising.

Research and Service

The method of accounting for research articles and service papers is, at best, very crude.* The quality of the papers, the contribution to the field, the prestige of the journal in which the
publication appears, the potential readership, and many other factors need to be given careful consideration before proper evaluation can be made. Fortunately, in most institutions such an
evaluation is made at the time of promotion or of tenured actions
and also annually in considering merit pay increases. For analysis
purposes, the number of research articles and number of service
papers are used as productivity measures and appear in the last
two columns.

*For this analysis, we counted papers given at national meetings as "service,"
although it is perhaps better to consider it an alternative measure of research
productivity.

MEASURING OVERALL PRODUCTIVITY

It is difficult to identify the programs that are either the "heavy" or "light" producers from the display format used in Table 7.1. Because of the spreadsheets now available for personal computers, it is possible to rank each program on any number of variables and to characterize that program as either heavy, medium, or light on each outcome variable and then relate these variables to one another. Based on the case study data in Table 7.1, this ranking and classification of programs have been done and are shown in Table 7.2. Table 7.2 allows us to make some comparisons between programs in terms of productivity.

The programs have been reordered in Table 7.2 based on the

Table 7.2
Ranks on Measures of Instructional Productivity by Program

PROGRAM	No. of FTE STUDENTS	STUDENT/ FACULTY RATIO	NO. OF MAJORS	TOTAL RANK SCORE	
11	3*	3	3	9	
13	3	3	3	9	
2	3	3	3	9	
10	3	3	3	9	HEAVY
3	3	2	3	8	
4	3	2	2	7	
17	2	3	2	7	
12	3	3	1	7	
1	2	1	3	6	
18	2	2	2	6	
19	2	2	2	6	
7	2	2	2	6	MEDIUM
5	2	2	1	5	
8	2	2	1	5	
6	1	2	2	5	
14	2	1	2	5	
9	1	2	2	4	
15	2	1	1	4	
20	1	2	1	4	LIGHT
21	1	1	1	3	
16	1	1	1	3	
22	1	1	1	3	

* 1 = Light, 2 = Medium, 3 = Heavy.

composite across the three instructional productivity rankings of FTES, student/faculty ratio, and number of majors, with the programs at the top having the greatest number of high rankings and those at the bottom having the greatest number of low rankings. The ranking were done only on measures of instruction and advisement, so the analysis represents only instructional productivity.

The ranking in the first column is based on the data in column 4 of Table 7.1 and represents program course enrollment in terms of full-time equivalent students (FTES). The ranking in the second column of Table 7.2 is based on the ratio of the data in columns 4 and 2 of Table 7.1 and represents full-time equivalent students taught in courses relative to number of faculty or student/faculty ratios. (Note that for 9 of the 22 programs, the rating for student enrollment [FTES] and the rating for student/faculty ratio are different.) Column 3 of Table 7.2 is based on the data in column 8 of Table 7.1 and represents the total number of majors across all three program levels. The last column of Table 7.2 is the sum of the three ranks that will be used as an indicator of a program's total instructional productivity. The FTES/FAC ratio establishes a weighting of individual faculty members' loads across programs.

We need to introduce the consideration here of whether or not the most productive programs are those that have the most or the fewest number of faculty members. There is no a priori reason to assume that a larger program would be more productive than a smaller program when the work load of each individual faculty member is considered. As we pursue this analysis, we will be able to answer questions about program size and individual faculty productivity.

When the 22 programs are rearranged in the order of composite instructional productivity as is done in Table 7.2, some indication of the relationship between size and productivity can be seen from the program numbers (based on the number of faculty as in Table 7.1) and their new positions (based on productivity). For example, program 1, which was number one in assigned faculty (remember that the program number is based on its relative position in terms of number of faculty), is now number nine in productivity, while program 12, which was number twelve in assigned faculty, is number seven in productivity.

CLASSIFYING PROGRAMS

To simplify the picture for purposes of making recommendations for organizational change, the data can be condensed another time. To accomplish this, the programs can be classified into groups based on their total instructional productivity score.

Table 7.3 displays all 22 programs categorized as either heavy, medium, or light in instructional productivity. These divisions are based on the analysis found in Table 7.2 and represent the composite or total rank score from the last column. As can be seen

Table 7.3
Program Classifications of Instructional Productivity Based on Number of Full-Time Equivalent Students, Faculty/Student Ratios, and Number of Majors Enrolled in a Given Semester

	All Levels	Undergrad & Masters	Graduate Only
Heavy	11 3 4 17	13	2 10 12
Medium	1 18		19 7 5 8 6 14
Light	9 15 20	21 22	16

from Table 7.3, all but three of the nine all-level programs are classified as medium or high in instructional productivity, while of the two-level and one-level programs, only four of the thirteen are high in instructional productivity. Thus, the flexibility gained by having all levels is a considerable advantage to a program as this analysis clearly demonstrates.

Unless a program has a relatively high demand, as is true of the three graduate-only programs and one master's plus undergraduate program classified here as heavy, it is difficult for a program that is purely or primarily graduate to maintain medium or higher instructional productivity. Programs that are relatively unproductive tend to be graduate-only programs and represent the great middle ground of a graduate and professional school, such as the college of education used in the case study.

DESCRIBING PROGRAM PRODUCTIVITY

Now, perhaps for the first time, it is possible to consider changes in the organizational chart that grow out of the analysis of instructional productivity by program. Table 7.4 relates the level of program productivity to the program input, process, and outcome measures described at the beginning of the chapter. The heavy, medium, and light designations come from Table 7.3. The per program measures of total number of faculty positions and number of full-time equivalent students are based on the data in Table 7.1. The per faculty measures of FTE students taught, number of majors advised, and number of articles published were schematized in the input, process, and outcome analysis presented in Figure 7.1.

There certainly exists the possibility that programs 9, 15, 16, 20, 21, and 22, those light in instructional productivity, are just too small to be productive. Three of those five programs have only two faculty members each, the only programs of the 22 with this small a number of faculty. (The other two have three faculty members each.) Discussions need to be held to see if some shifting of faculty to related program areas (for example, science shifted to mathematics in order to form a mathematics/science and computers program) might provide the critical mass needed to allow individual faculty members to devote more time to a role in a larger program

Table 7.4
Outcome Measures for Programs and Faculty in Three Productivity Level Groups

| | Per Program Measures | | | | | Per Program Measures | | | |
| | | | | | | Teacher | Adviser | Research | Service |
Instructional Productivity Group	Total Faculty	Number of Programs	Number of Instructional Faculty (FTE)	% of Teaching Assistants	Student Credit Hours	Student Credit Hours	Majors Advised	Articles Published	Papers Presented
Heavy	55	8	7	70	70	219	17	7	10
Medium	36	8	4.5	25	25	157	12	6	10
Light	20	6	3	5	5	108	10	4	3

for which they are specially suited rather than being required to continue to play all of the roles in one small program. Other explanations of the difference in productivity by program need to be explored. For example, the different use of graduate teaching assistant funds, differences in national demands for program graduates, or contributions of missions to the institution all need to be examined as they affect the instructional productivity of programs.

It is interesting to note from Table 7.4 that other than for the weak programs, which average about 2.5 faculty members each, the remaining programs—regardless of either instructional productivity or research productivity—average about 5.5 faculty members each. Given essentially the same number of faculty members, the strong programs are generating at least twice as many FTE students in instruction, almost three times as many majors, and the same amount of research as their counterparts in the light to medium range. Thus, the strong programs are truly "strong" relative to all of the organizational goals.

DECISION MAKING

The strong programs are clearly the high payoff programs and should be the prime candidates for expansion, while the light programs would seem to lack either the critical faculty mass or the student market to remain viable. If a reorganization were to be done, it would have to focus on achieving a greater equalization in instructional productivity across programs. At the very least, the weak programs should be incorporated into stronger ones or allowed to disappear through attrition.

It is clear that some programs are just too small and too unproductive to remain a single program unit. Of the weak programs, programs 16, 20, and 21 were good candidates to be eliminated or to be combined with other programs into a general area (like policy analysis). Many of the faculty members in these three programs will retire in the next five years, and this analysis will help justify a reallocation of those lines to other programs. Program 22 represents a vital area for the college and should get additional funds and positions combined with intense efforts to recruit more students. Program 15 would join a larger unit and concentrate on a general area within the college. Among the very strong programs, program 10 needed to be reviewed to see if it was consistent with the mission of the college. It is clearly understaffed and the large infusion of funds needed may be better spent on other programs.

A university is a service organization and the primary clients it serves are students. When parts of that organization utilize resources but have few clients for those resources, then necessary resources are drawn away from the more productive units. Although program enrollments will tend to vary across extended periods of time, the kind of misfit between resource allocations and enrollments reflected in this instructional productivity analysis can be expected to cripple an organization.

Only after careful consideration and open debate of all relevant issues should change be considered regarding the organizational chart. It would be useful to ask department heads and chairpersons of key faculty committees, after receiving the instructional productivity analysis, to consider the following challenge in order to bring out some of the major substantive issues involved in organizational change. Some guidelines representing the application of outcome management might include the following:

1. Reduce the number of programs from 22 to approximately 15 with about 8 faculty members in each program. Currently the most productive programs are the first 15 that appear in Table 7.3 and the least productive are the remaining 7. Seven programs could be either eliminated or combined with other programs over a five-year period.

2. Select five programs that are most likely to profit from additional funding and five that can be maintained without additional funding.

3. If the final selection is based on criteria other than productivity, specify what criteria were used.

4. For each program, indicate what additional knowledge, insights, or judgments were made about the continuing development of that program and how this relates to productivity.

We expect, at the end, to have fewer programs (closer to 10 than to 20), fewer faculty positions (half-time retired faculty members will not be replaced), and a less ambitious curriculum. We will try to create an organizational chart that reflects a few (say three or four) major missions and several (again three or four) programs those missions support.

MAKING OTHER DECISIONS BASED ON PRODUCTIVITY

Other productivity analyses may be performed in order to evaluate academic programs. There are various questions that need further clarification in order to understand the relationship between the assignment of faculty time and productivity. The following example taken from the case study led to an inquiry into and review of a college practice that was not consistent within or between programs.

We found the conventional wisdom that "the typical teaching load per faculty member is two courses for six credits per term" to be incorrect. Consider the data from two programs, A and B, shown in Table 7.5, based on the individual teaching and advising loads shown in Table 7.6.

Table 7.5
A Comparison of Teaching Loads in Two Programs

	Program A	Program B
Number of courses	7	7
Number of credits	21	21
Number of faculty	4	2
% of instruction	3.2*	1.3*
Number of students	31	39
No.of students per instructor	10	30

*Number of full-time equivalent instructional faculty.

Table 7.6
A Comparison of Teaching Loads for Faculty in Two Programs

	% Inst.	No. of Courses Taught	No. of Credits Taught	No. of Students Taught	SCH.	FTES	PhDs	FTES
Program A								
Prof. A	80	2	6	20	120	10.0	1	0.2
Prof. B	80	2	6	18	84	7.0	9	1.8
Prof. C	70	1	3	14	42	3.5	2	0.3
Prof. D	90	2	6	21	126	10.5	0	0
Total	**3.2***	**7**	**21**	**73**	**372**	**31.0**	**12**	**2.3**
Program B								
Prof. E	70	3	11	83	326	21.7	0	0
Prof. F	58	4	10	94	255	17.0	0	0
Total	**1.3***	**7**	**21**	**177**	**581**	**38.7**	**0**	**0**

*Number of full-time equivalent instructional faculty.

The teaching load differences in the two programs produce a number of FTE faculty which, when divided by the number of FTE students, yields a ratio that is three times larger in program B than in program A. In other words, program B produces three times more FTE students per FTE faculty member than program A. Obviously, if a professor in program A should retire, it would be inconsistent with outcome management to return the position to program A. It might be more productive to move the position to program B.

CONCLUSION

And so we have come full circle. We have identified a basis for making changes in the organizational chart: being careful consideration of the productivity and assignments of faculty members. We are not recommending that the analysis make the decisions.

The decisions must be made by people with experience, expert knowledge, and personal understanding of the complexity of an organization's structure. But those people should be provided with information about the productivity of units within that structure relative to the resources devoted to each unit.

Outcome management calls for a focus on outcomes and the plans for their attainment as the basis for allocating resources. Instructional productivity is one of the most important outcomes, particularly in relation to the existing distribution of resources, since this forms the basis for the determination of efficiency, one of the three organizational goals. To maximize efficiency, resources should be redistributed away from the least productive units into the most productive ones. In this chapter we have presented a series of analyses demonstrating how the necessary determinations can be made for allocating resources to programs.

8

Rewards and Productivity

An important aspect of the outcome management model is the association or link between rewards and productivity. In order to maximize the productivity of either an individual or a group, there must be some tangible gain for the individual or group that clearly results from the productive efforts. It is helpful to provide performers with more than the mere satisfaction of accomplishment. That something more in our socioeconomic system is money.

In some institutions of higher education, annual salary increments are based on a schedule that eliminates the possibility of using raises as a differentiated reward. However, in the majority of institutions, salary raises are based on the discretion or judgment of administrators. That judgment may be based on merit considerations, equity considerations, political considerations, or some combination of the three.

In the first part of this chapter, we will look at salaries in one college of a university, as a case study, and attempt to determine the degree to which they varied according to faculty productivity. That is, we will see whether and to what degree rewards were linked to productivity over a recent five-year period. The second part of this chapter describes a system and procedure used in the sample college to distribute discretionary raises as a function of productivity. The third part of this chapter examines the results of the systematic distribution plan and the relationship between these results and those of a concomitant system of basing raises on peer judgments of merit.

THE EXISTING LINK BETWEEN SALARY AND PRODUCTIVITY

The determinants of academic salaries have been studied at various levels. Tolles and Melichar (1968) used large samples of several hundred institutions in order to determine the variables involved in academic salary. The years of experience of the individual faculty member and the characteristics of the institution seemed to account for most of the differences. Institutional differences related to the type of institution (university, private, independent, church), geographic location, proportion of students pursuing graduate or professional degrees, and percentage of faculty holding the rank of full professor.

Other researchers have studied individual institutions. Katz (1973), Koch and Chizmar (1973), and Ferber and Kordick (1978) looked at several hundred employees within an institution and replicated some of the findings from studies across institutions. Significant predictors of faculty salaries included faculty experience and number of journal publications. It also appears that there are differences among departments, with the sciences and professions getting higher salaries than the humanities (Tuckman & Hageman, 1976; Siegfried & White, 1973).

At the individual institutional level, the factors that affect promotion, tenure, and individual faculty member salary raises can be determined. Typically these are discussed in terms of faculty assignment for research, teaching, and service as well as productivity in terms of number of articles, number of books, amount of teaching, and public service performed.

Saupe (1978) has pointed out the difficulties with many studies of faculty salary due to inadequate data bases and difficulties inherent in measuring teaching ability, scholarship, and service. Yet the power to reward faculty members has a significant effect on performance (Kallenberg & Sorenson, 1979). Institutional researchers continue to investigate faculty salary issues because most of the money spent annually for higher education goes to faculty salaries and discretionary increases may be one of the few remaining ways to motivate an increasingly tenured faculty.

In this section we will build on previous findings in order to describe the variables that tend to make a difference in salaries and salary raises, in both absolute and relative terms, and to discuss some of the relationships among those variables. We will also attempt to identify the issues that administrators must consider in allocating discretionary salary dollars.

DO SALARIES AND PRODUCTIVITY RELATE?

The general approach used to describe the marketplace structure for salaries at a single institution was to examine the salaries over the past five years of 83 full-time faculty members in one college of one state university. These salaries were examined in relationship to 30 variables having to do with the general areas of experience; percentage of time assigned to instruction; instructional productivity in terms of student credit hours taught; research and service productivity in terms of publications, research grants, professional leadership positions, and advising, and two demographic variables of sex and race.

Those of the 125 faculty members in the college who held administrative posts, half-time appointments due to partial retirement, were on leave for sabbatical or other purposes, or were temporary faculty were excluded.

The data used for this case study came from the faculty activity report, the faculty vitas, the faculty payroll records, and the listing of contracts and grants.

The faculty activity report was compiled at the end of the fall 1984 semester on each faculty member and included the percentage of time assigned to teaching, to research, and to service; the courses taught per level (graduate, undergraduate); the number of credits and the number of students in each course; the number of students in variable credit courses (directed independent study, comprehensive examinations, dissertation advising); and the names of students for which the individual faculty member served as major professor.

The second data source was the faculty members' vitas. From this document the following information was collected for the past five years: number of articles published in scholarly journals, books written, monographs written, papers presented at national meetings, and portion of the total publications that were classified by the individual faculty members as either research, scholarly, or creative.

The third data source was the payroll record for the past five years, from which was established the following variables: salary, amount of discretionary (merit) salary increases, ratio of salary increases to total salary, year of employment, year of birth, and race and sex of each faculty member.

Lists of contracts and grants in force provided data on the number of grants an individual faculty member held at any given time.

Regression analyses of salary, raises, and their ratios were done to reduce the number of variables by selecting those that accounted for the largest amount of variance. The purpose of regression analysis is to discover the degree to which each of a set of variables in combination predicts an outcome (Glass & Hopkins, 1984). If the variables predict an outcome perfectly, a value of 1.00 is obtained; if they do not predict it at all, zero is the result. The aim was to determine which variables predicted faculty salaries, raises, and the ratio of salary to raises. Based on the results of these regression analyses, the following variables were identified as predictors of faculty financial status: rank of faculty members (as a measure of experience), graduate student credit hours taught (as a measure of teaching), number of journal articles (a measure of publications), contracts and grants held (a measure of research), and the number of Ph.D.s advised (as a measure of advising). The results are shown in Table 8.1 and Figure 8.1.

With total current salary as the dependent variable (or outcome to be predicted), experience (in the form of rank) accounted for most of the variance (that is, it was the best predictor by far). This was to be expected even in a marketplace system where the faculty members who have the most experience tended to receive the

Table 8.1
Regression Analyses of Five Independent Variables and the Dependent Variables of (1) 1984–85 Salary, (2) 1979–85 Merit Pay, and (3) the Ratio of (2) Divided by (1) for 83 Faculty Members

Independent Variable	(1) Salary		(2) Merit Pay		(3) Ratio	
	Simple r	Mult. r	Simple r	Mult. r	Simple r	Mult. r
Experience	.75***	.75	.30*	.30	.01	.01
Teaching	.18	.76	.27	.39	.25*	.26
Publication	-.08	.76	.11	.42	.21*	.34
Research	.16	.77	.21	.45	.20*	.39
Advising	.52***	.81	.44**	.56	.26*	.46

$*p < .05$, $**p < .01$, $***p < .001$

Figure 8.1
The Degree to Which Faculty Performance Variables Predict Salary,
Merit Raises, and Their Ratios

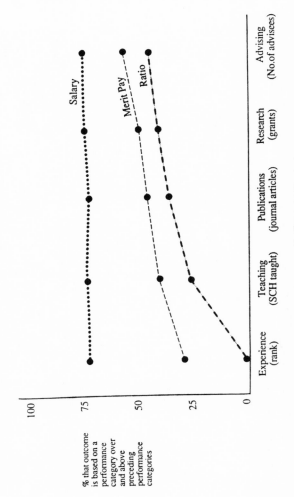

highest salaries. Notice in Figure 8.1 that the plot for salary is almost perfectly horizontal. After experience or rank is taken as a basis for total salary, none of the other categories adds much to the picture.

The second analysis was run with merit as the dependent variable or outcome, but again, as can be seen from Table 8.1, experience accounted for most of the variance. In Figure 8.1, the plot for merit pay is again somewhat horizontal and rises very little after experience or rank is taken into account. However, merit pay is much less predictable than salary. This analysis ran counter to the belief that merit pay was awarded for meritorious work, whether done by a junior or senior faculty member. Since, by contract, merit pay must be allocated in units that represent 1.75 percent of a faculty member's total salary (called half-steps), a bias is introduced into the results. A faculty member who makes $50,000 a year gets more money for a half-step than a faculty member who makes $20,000 a year.

The third analysis involved a possible correction for the influence of rank on both merit pay and salary. The correction was accomplished by dividing the merit pay by the total salary. The result of using this ratio as the outcome or dependent variable (column 3, Ratio, in Table 8.1) is that the predictor of rank or experience no longer accounts for any significant variance, while the four remaining performance factors account for a significant proportion of the variability in awarding of merit pay relative to salary. Look at the ratio line in Figure 8.1. It is the most stepwise of the three and starts almost at zero. It does not end as high as the salary line, which means that the ratio is less predictable than salary, but more of the performance factors play a role in predicting the ratio than in predicting salary.

The results lead us to two conclusions. First, financial rewards must be conceived of as units that represent a fixed percentage of total salary but a variable amount of dollars in order for them to be independent of rank and experience. To accomplish this, we will continue to use the half-step unit, which represents a 1.75 percent increase in salary. The higher the faculty member's salary base, the greater will be the absolute magnitude of the raise even though the percentage remains constant. In the absence of a system that awards raises in constant units of dollars, we must continue to rely on a fixed percentage unit in order to have results that are independent of rank.

The second conclusion is that even though merit raises at the college were not formally and systematically awarded on the basis of productivity, they did tend to reflect productivity in the areas of instruction and research. Those faculty members who tended to teach and advise more students and who carried out and published more research were more likely to receive raises than those who tended to do less. The magnitude of the relationships was not great, even when considered cumulatively. A multiple correlation of .46 indicates that only about one-quarter of the variation in salary raise units can be explained or predicted by the combined productivity measures.

A SYSTEM FOR DISTRIBUTING RAISES ON THE BASIS OF PRODUCTIVITY

Two separate systems were established at the college in the year following the period used in the preceding analysis to distribute salary raises. One of these systems was based on peer judgments and the raises allocated on this basis were called merit raises. Each academic department had its own procedures for allocating these raises but they tended to have two features in common. One feature was that they were based on peer review, judgment, and recommendations. The second feature was that the principle data used for making the judgments were ostensibly productivity data with the heaviest emphasis on research productivity (i.e., refereed journal publications).

The second system used to distribute salary raises, and the one on which we will place most focus, was based on administrative judgment and resulted in allocations called discretionary raises. The two systems of merit raises and discretionary raises used in the given year represent a division of what was formerly a single system from which the data set presented at the beginning of this chapter was obtained.

A formal system was created by the central administration of the college for allocating discretionary raises in the given year. It was based on a set of three, equally weighted ratings, one for instructional productivity, one for research productivity, and one for service productivity. The system is shown in Table 8.2. The discretionary raise system weights the three productivity areas equally by using the formula:

$$\text{Overall Rating} = \text{Rating for Instruction} + \text{Rating for Research} + \text{Rating for Service}$$

The rating for instruction is obtained by summing the rating for student credit hours generated with the rating for number of doctoral student advisees and dividing by two. Instructional productivity, therefore, is considered to be equally a function of class instruction and individual advisement. Faculty members in departments with large undergraduate programs and small graduate programs tend to do better in amount of class instruction than in advisement, while for those in largely graduate departments, the reverse is true.

The rating for research is obtained by summing the rating for journal publications with the rating for number of contracts and grants and dividing by two. Because of the length of time required to produce a journal article and have it published, this measure was rated over a five-year as opposed to a one-year period.

The rating for service was based on the judgments of the three highest ranking members of the college's central administration and reflected on their perceptions of individual willingness to work for or against college goals.

The overall ratings for each member of the entire faculty of the college were computed based on the formula given above, and these overall ratings were then rank-ordered and subdivided into three categories: high, middle, and low. The high category represented the most productive group of faculty members, and the low category represented the least productive group.

ACTUAL RAISE ALLOCATIONS USING TWO SYSTEMS

The discretionary raise system described above represents one where outcome management would operate in its pure form. That is, rewards would be linked to productivity alone and hence greater productivity would be accompanied by greater rewards. However,

Table 8.2
Basis for Ratings of College Faculty Members for Discretionary Salary Raises in the Given Year

| Rating | INSTRUCTION | | RESEARCH | | SERVICE |
	No. of Student Credit Hours Taught	No. of Active Doctoral Advisees	No. of Journal Articles Published (last 5 years)	Current No. of Contracts and Grants	Administrative Rating of Contribution to College Goals
1	395 + (20%)*	5 - 11 (11%)	5 (10%)	4 + (13%)	Strong (25%)
2	295 - 394 (20%)	3 - 4 (14%)	3 - 4 (15%)	3 (8%)	Positive (15%)
3	195 - 294 (20%)	2 (10%)	2 (10%)	2 (7%)	None (37%)
4	95 - 194 (20%)	1 (15%)	1 (15%)	1 (25%)	Negative (13%)
5	0 - 94 (20%)	0 (50%)	0 (50%)	0 (47%)	Detracts (10%)

* Numbers in parentheses represent the percentage of faculty members receiving a given rating.

in the operation of the actual system in the college, the department heads were asked to prepare a list of faculty members whom they would recommend for discretionary raises based on their perceptions of service to the department. The judgment of department heads, however, tended to be based, at least in part, on trying to gain support from selected individuals. Department heads also were aware of the results of the merit ratings made by their faculty and could have been biased to use the discretionary raises as an opportunity to reward some faculty members not otherwise recognized by their peers.

At any rate, the resulting distribution of discretionary raises did not conform exactly to the system described in the previous section. The discrepancy between the distribution of faculty who would have received discretionary raises under the pure system but did not or who would not have received discretionary raises under the pure system but did is about 10 percent. On this basis, the system can be said to have operated reasonably close to its pure form.

Both systems used the half-step (1.75 percent of base salary) as the unit of allocation. Each system was carried out totally independently of the other. The number of merit raise half-steps awarded in the given year in question was 77, while the number of discretionary raise half-steps awarded was 62. The resulting distribution of raises of the two systems combined in the given year is shown below.

Number of half-steps	% of increase	Number of faculty
0	0	25
1	1.75%	40
2	3.50%	36
3	5.25%	9

RESULTS OF THE SYSTEMS ALONE AND IN COMBINATION

Of the 62 faculty members awarded discretionary raises, 11 were not rated and ranked because they were only half-time or were on leave. Of the remaining 51 discretionary raises, slightly over half were given to faculty members rated high on productivity, with the remaining distributed among those rated middle or low. The result of the distribution of discretionary raises is shown in Table 8.3.

Table 8.3
Distribution of Discretionary Raises by Ranking

	(High) 1-2	(Middle) 3	(Low) 4-5
RAISE	26	8	17
NO RAISE	7	13	30

RANKING

PHI = .42 (without the middle column)

In order to establish the degree of predictability of getting a raise, given one's productivity (that is, the correspondence between faculty performance and the allocation of raises), a phi coefficient was computed among those rated high and those rated low on productivity. (The middle group was eliminated because a phi coefficient can only be computed on a 2 × 2 classification table.) The magnitude of the phi coefficient reflects the extent to which high performers were given raises and low performers not. A perfect correspondence would yield a value of 1.00 and no correspondence, zero. For discretionary raises based on the outcome management system, a phi coefficient of .42 was obtained.

Of the 77 faculty members awarded merit raises, 75 had been rated on productivity with only slightly more than a third having received high ratings. The result of the distribution of merit raises is shown in Table 8.4. The phi coefficient relating merit raises to productivity amounted to only .15.

A third analysis was done on the results of the two systems of raise allocation in combination. The distribution of faculty at each

Table 8.4
Distribution of Merit Raises by Ranking

	RANKING		
	(High) 1-2	(Middle) 3	(Low) 4-5
RAISE	26	16	32
NO RAISE	5	5	13

PHI = .15 (without the middle column)

of the five levels of productivity relative to the exact number of half-step raises obtained by each is shown in Table 8.5. This was then reduced to the 2 × 3 contingency table format used in the previous analyses and appears in Table 8.6. Of the 44 faculty members who received either two or three half-step raises, exactly half were ranked high on productivity. The resulting phi coefficient was .40.

A comparison of the two allocation systems alone and in combination is shown in Figure 8.2. From the figure, it is apparent that the merit raise system was not nearly as performance-based as the discretionary raise system.

A number of conclusions can be drawn from the results. The first is that judgments that were more data-based did, in fact, yield results that were more closely related to actual productivity. Peer evaluations were less data-based than the discretionary raise procedures used by the administrators.

The problem with the peer evaluation approach can be laid at the doorstep of department heads rather than the faculty themselves. Faculty committees rated and ranked their peers on productivity and transmitted these judgments to their department heads. Department heads then used them to allocate merit raises. Department heads allocated raises by starting at the top of the recommended list and working downward. Since they gave each

Table 8.5
Distribution of Total Raises by Ranking

			RANKING			
		(High)				(Low)
		1	2	3	4	5
Size of Raise (Number of Half-Steps)	3	4	0	3	1	0
	2	11	7	5	6	7
	1	1	6	8	10	8
	0	2	1	5	6	11

person no more than one half-step raise, they were able to go quite far down their list. After giving one half-step raise to three-quarters of their faculty, the relationship between productivity, as judged by peers, and receiving a raise was quite small (remember the phi of .15).

Had department heads awarded two half-steps to their highest rated group and none to their lowest rated group, the faculty-judgment-based merit system would have related strongly to productivity. However, department heads were perhaps more motivated to spread the rewards around rather than distribute them "on target." In terms of outcome management, this widespread distribution is a poor strategy. In terms of avoiding complaints from nonproductive faculty, it probably is a good one.

It is also worth noting that the discretionary allocation would have been more closely associated with productivity had it not been for the role of the department heads who tended to "nominate" almost as many faculty members for raises who were low on productivity as those high. In this case, their recommendations may have served a clear political purpose at the department level but one that was unrelated to the management of productivity outcomes.

Table 8.6
Accumulated Distribution of Total Raises by Ranking

		RANKING		
		(High)	(Middle)	(Low)
		1-2	3	4-5
Size of Raise (Number of Half-Steps)	2-3	22	8	14
	0-1	10	13	35

PHI = .40 (without the middle column)

Recall from earlier in the chapter that a multiple correlation of .46 was obtained between productivity indicators and percentage increase in salary over the past five years (prior to last year). Last year, in spite of an attempt to relate rewards to productivity more systematically, their relationship only achieved .40. This suggests two conclusions. The first is that rewards are indeed based on productivity, at least in part, regardless of whether the reward/no reward judgment is based on peer review or administrative review. The second is that rewards are based on factors other than productivity at least to the same degree as they are on productivity.

If we subscribe to the outcome management model, which includes a built-in relationship between desired outcomes and rewards, we must conclude that there are desired outcomes in operation that rival, if not surpass, those subsumed under the heading of productivity, and that these other outcomes are particularly desired by administrators, particularly department heads. These other, nonproductivity outcomes can be considered political in that they relate to the popularity and ultimately the power of the department head and are maximized by using raise dollars to overcome opposition, win over new allies, and generally minimize complaints among those whose complaining may be both threatening and likely.

Figure 8.2
A Comparison of the Reward Allocation Systems in Terms of Their Correspondence to Faculty Performance

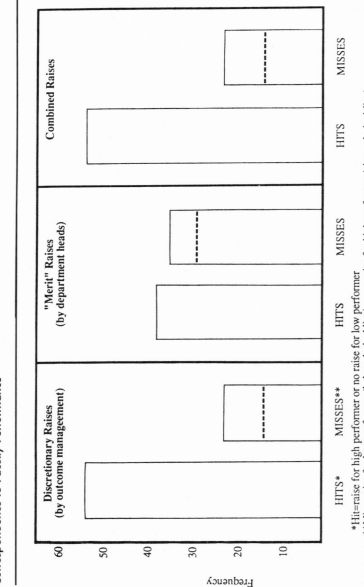

*Hit=raise for high performer or no raise for low performer
**Miss=raise for low performer (below dashed line) or no raise for high performer (above dashed line)

Hence, our case study has taken us to a point where we can perhaps better understand and evaluate the outcome management approach as a strategy for increasing productivity among college faculty.

9

The Bottom Line

Outcome management is a model for directing an organization that focuses on using resources to help the organization meet its goals. Its use requires that organizational goals be set, that performance on measures of goal attainment be monitored, and that contributions to organizational goal attainment be the basis for rewards and resource allocations.

The model was implemented in the case of a large college of education with the goals of recognition, responsiveness, and efficiency. A management information system was put in place to measure productivity in instruction, research, and service at the individual and at the program levels. Instructional productivity focused on the number of student credit hours generated and the number of majors. Research productivity focused on the number of publications generated per faculty member. Service focused on direct contributions to the organization.

In order to enhance the likelihood that resource allocations would yield goal attainment, a planning process was undertaken at individual, program, and collegewide levels. The purpose of planning was to set forth a series of intended actions to guide the goal attainment process. Individual and program consequences were attached to the various plans that were developed to ensure that the planning process was more than an exercise.

Decisions regarding the allocation of resources were based on individual and program performance relative to desired goals. The distribution of vacant positions or lines to programs could be projected as a function of the instructional productivity of each program relative to the size of its current faculty. At the individual level, end-of-year discretionary raises were allocated to faculty on the basis of actual performances in instruction, research, and service, with instruction being defined in the same quantitative terms as the other goal areas.

What can we now say about the outcome management model as a decision-making tool? Its use raised a number of issues, both substantive and evaluative. It helped to crystallize a number of issues that are critical to the functioning of an effective organization in higher education. We will first turn to those issues and discuss them in the light of the model and the case study.

DECISION-MAKING FOCUS: CURRICULUM VS. CLIENTELE

A major set of decisions is made prior to each semester when the schedule of classes to be offered is put together. This schedule is a blueprint for the allocation of existing organizational resources to instruction. It is heavily influenced by the curriculum that is required for degree attainment in the various programs offered by the organization. In other words, the projected class schedule is largely curriculum-driven. That is, if a program exists, then its curriculum must be sequentially offered so that the curriculum can be completed by students.

From an outcome management perspective, the class schedule should be determined by the clientele, that is, the students, based on their selection of courses to take. This is true because the organizational goal of efficiency requires a match or correspondence between student needs and course offerings so that course enrollments can be maximized. The goal would be a minimum number of students enrolled in each and every course, that number being sufficient to make each course self-sufficient.

To some extent the course schedule will be the same whether or not the course schedule is curriculum-driven or enrollment-driven because students are required to complete curriculum sequences in order to gain degrees. In other words, students cannot and will not simply select any course they want; they will take courses they must have and this is determined by the curriculum.

However, there are many curriculums because there are many programs, and each curriculum will have its required courses. Programs that have few majors will not have students to enroll in their required courses, while programs that have many majors will have students to enroll. The first inevitable area of decision raised by outcome management is the absolute necessity to eliminate programs that have too few students to maintain fully enrolled required courses.

This issue will be exacerbated when faculty members, who are responsible for the curriculum, increase the requirements for program completion. Such course proliferation, often in the guise of raising standards, only creates more teaching assignments and spreads an already thin student body even thinner.

DECISION-MAKING LOCUS: FACULTY CHOICE
VS. CLIENTELE CHOICE

A variation on the above theme occurs in the area of elective courses. Faculty members often choose the courses they want to teach and those are the ones that are offered. Moreover, faculty members will often choose to teach electives and leave required courses to be taught by graduate students and adjuncts who are paid out of annual budget funds to deliver the necessary instruction. Occasionally, faculty members will receive reduced loads and their teaching assignments will then be taken over in whole or in part by paid instructors.

Where a faculty member opts to teach an esoteric course, that course will either run with a small enrollment or not at all; in the latter instance, the faculty member may not be given an alternate teaching assignment if none is available or acceptable.

The net result is that the class schedule may be more a function of faculty choice than of student demand but student demand can only be bent so far. What happens is that the difference between faculty choice and student demand is made up by courses taught by graduate students, adjuncts, and, occasionally, faculty paid on an overload basis. In other words, budget is required to offer the courses you need so that faculty can teach the courses they want.

BALANCING THE SYSTEM BY DESIRED OUTCOMES

Outcome management prescribes that the class schedule be based on student enrollments rather than on either curriculum requirements or faculty teaching choices. Since student enrollments will always be a reflection, in part, of both curriculum requirements and faculty teaching choices, these factors will be satisfied to the degree that the system can tolerate. Going beyond what the system can handle is costly and should be avoided. Instead, other strategies can be incorporated into plans such as recruiting more students, or changing the size or composition of the faculty, or offering larger sections, or giving faculty members heavier teaching loads.

The current procedure for creating the class schedule may be too oriented toward meeting individual faculty needs and not oriented enough toward meeting the needs of the organization. The needs of the organization in the outcome management approach are specified as organizational goals. Where one of these goals focuses on efficiency, then the class schedule must maximize student enrollment at an affordable cost. Affordability may demand a change in previously accepted faculty practices.

CHANGING THE PAYOFF STRUCTURE

Organizational goals will be most easily met, according to outcome management, when they correspond to individual goals. One way to increase the likelihood of meeting the organizational goal of affordable instruction would be to make instructional productivity pay off for individual faculty members. Given the use of outcome management for resource allocation, this should not be difficult to accomplish. Give the programs that generate the most student credit hours per full-time equivalent faculty member the new lines and give the faculty members who individually teach the most student credit hours the raises and it will not be long before faculty value systems will change to reflect these new bases for payoff.

A similar argument can be made for the allocation of research time. Rather than giving everyone research time, outcome management would say that research time should be a payoff for research productivity and should go, therefore, to the productive researchers.

SPECIALIZATION VS. GENERALIZATION

Organizational goals are more easily met when there is some degree of flexibility and overlap between the members of the organization. Outcome management would call for an increase in generalization and a decrease in specialization among regular, full-time faculty members. This would increase the likelihood that required courses could be covered by existing faculty. It would also make it easier to deal with short-term enrollment fluctuations between programs because faculty members, with general skills and knowledge, could teach basic courses in more than one program area.

Specialization, on the other hand, is costly for an organization to maintain. In a research college or university, every faculty member is a specialist, so graduate students are often left to teach the undergraduate program. If, in return for this concentration of specialists, the organization is able more readily to attain its goal of recognition while being able, at the same time, to meet its other goals, this specialization would be not only acceptable but appropriate. However, more often than not, this heightened specialization may do the organization relatively little good in terms of meeting any of its goals and may be very costly as well. For most colleges and universities, generalization and overlap are likely to be an organizational strategy more conducive to goal attainment than specialization.

POPULARITY: PRODUCERS VS. POLITICIANS

Are we dealing with a situation of inevitable and irreconcilable differences? Will all faculty members be at odds with organizational goals and the behaviors necessary to attain them within the context of outcome management? Is there an unavoidable gap between the outcomes that faculty members desire for themselves and those that benefit the institution of which those faculty members are a part?

To answer this question, we looked at the results of the case study and identified two groups of faculty who can be labeled producers and politicians. (This categorization scheme also applies equally well to administrators, as we shall see.) Producers are faculty members who devote their time and effort to teaching, research, and service and produce student credit hours, publications, and completed service contracts. Politicians are faculty members who devote their time and effort to establishing and maintaining political connections with other faculty members and administrators that constitute a source of power or influence. There is also a third group of faculty, whom we call disengagers, who are neither productive nor political. This group basically avoids any real engagement in either their faculty career or in the institution for which they work. (At the extreme of this third group is even a fourth small group who cannot manage to stay out of real trouble—usually with drugs, alcohol, students, or the law—and might be called deviants.)

The reaction by producers to an outcome management system is positive. Since outcome management recognizes and rewards productivity, the producers suddenly find themselves in a favorable situation. Perhaps for the first time, their productive efforts are noted and noteworthy and they are distinguished from their peers on that basis. The reaction by politicians to an outcome management system is negative. Politicians now find themselves in what for them is a strange situation. They cannot alter the consequences of behavior through the use of political power since those consequences are linked to performance outcomes and not to political connections.

The producers are not only positive, they also become even more productive because they are now receiving both encouragement and resources. In the past they produced even though they were treated the same as everyone else. Now they are treated better and produce even more. The politicians also increase their behavior, but their behavior is political. Even though they can expect to gain through productivity, they continue to behave politically—perhaps for two reasons. First, they do not have the talents and skills that productivity requires and so it would be too demanding for them. Second, being political is what they are good at and so they continue it. But they do more than continue it; they intensify it. And the reason for this is that they are threatened by the demands and by the potential loss of power imposed by outcome management and so they must politic with a purpose—to stamp out outcome management.

What is likely to happen? The producers produce more and the politicians politic more. What the producers produce increases the effectiveness of outcome management. What the politicians politic for is to bring an end to outcome management. They claim that outcome management is mechanistic and inhumane and focuses on trivial outcomes and is exploitive of the faculty. They resist and take issue at efforts for faculty planning and at all aspects of the data collection process. They suggest that the operation of outcome management is dictatorial, tyrannical, and secretive.

But none of these claims is true. Outcome management is as much driven and directed by productive faculty members as is a political approach to management by political faculty members. In fact, outcome management is more open and honest because it operates according to a public set of rules, which means that all decisions can be made and justified in public. Outcome management is exactly what it seems to be, nothing more and nothing less. Moreover, it is a technique for managing an organization that is pro-organization, that is, that publicly and openly attempts to further the organization. Politically oriented management systems, alternatively, favor the needs of selected faculty members, those with political power, and usually at the expense of the organization.

To the extent that outcome management does not allow disengagement with a high degree of comfort, the third faculty group, the disengagers may be drawn in to take sides and may then be expected to side with the politicians.

CAN OUTCOME MANAGEMENT BE MADE TO WORK?

There is no question about either the potential for outcome management to work in higher education or its effectiveness in increasing the efficiency with which an institution spends its money. Even within the short two-year span of the case study, there was a noticeable upward trend in the number of student credit hours being taught by each faculty member. Because outcome management is so focused on a target or targets, it can dramatically increase the number of decision-making hits relative to misses.

The more telling question is whether outcome management will be allowed to work by a higher education community that is much more accustomed to a politically oriented decision-making system and to having decisions made in private. What follows are a set of requirements whose presence would auger well for the success of outcome management.

Hard Financial Times. When the money flow into higher education is low and the public expectation for performance high, a targeted, overt decision-making system like outcome management has its best chance to succeed. This is true because budget-cutting, program elimination, and reallocation of resources will all become necessary and will all put pressure on a politically oriented decision-making system. Faculty and administration will then be less reluctant to accept an open set of rules to cover the cutback process.

A Less Politicized System. Some institutions have more well-defined and powerful political elites or factions and so vested interests will be high. In these institutions, it will be hard for a nonpolitical decision-making system to have a real chance to take hold because it will threaten too many "empires" and because the power will exist to undermine it. The existence of powerful unions or a powerful senate is usually an indication that a system is too politicized for outcome management to work.

Reinforcement and Support at the Top. The uppermost leadership of an institution must make a commitment to a system such as outcome management for even a segment of the total institution in order for it to be likely to work. Operating an institution or a unit within it under a new system with public access to information and unavoidable consequences of member actions is likely to produce some level of conflict, particularly in its formative stages. University presidents must be secure enough and prepared to allow this conflict to dissipate itself rather than reacting to it and becoming part of it.

Involvement and Commitment by Productive Faculty. The major source of support for outcome management must come from faculty, and productive faculty represent its potential support base. Productive faculty are the ones who will see the benefits not only to the organization as a whole but to them as well, since productivity is the very outcome that outcome management attempts to maximize. Since resources will be allocated to productive programs and productive faculty, these must provide the backbone of support. However, such productive faculty members are unaccustomed to playing an influential organizational role. Their time is usually spent in productive work and they characteristically leave organizational management issues to the politicians, who have the most time and the most zeal for the intrigue required to operate a typically political system.

For this reason, gaining the involvement and commitment of productive faculty will require a systematic and sustained effort by administration. Productive faculty should be identified and organized to form a management advisory committee. This committee should be involved not only in frequent communication with administration but should also play a truly managerial role in the operation of all facets of outcome management, including goal setting, identification and collection of data, planning, and allocation of resources—both to programs and to individuals.

It is important to realize that support and involvement in operating the system may not come from first-level managers such as department heads since these people may be too committed to maintaining their own political position, particularly if it depends on the support of faculty. In other words, do not attempt to use an existing political subsystem to maintain outcome management since the two may be mutually incompatible. Instead, create a new governance mechanism that employs productive faculty members in a management role, even though such a role may be unfamiliar to many of them. It will undoubtedly take a good bit of selling on your part to get these faculty members to play this role.

Determination and Willingness to Innovate. He or she who at-

tempts to lead a higher education organization by means of outcome management must be an innovator and must accept the risks
associated with breaking new ground. However, if you believe that
the ultimate effectiveness of organizations requires that they attempt to maximize their productivity, and that to do so, resources
must be allocated accordingly, it will be difficult for you to manage
any other way. In fact, to be an outcome manager, you yourself
must be a productive faculty member, and few productive faculty
members either choose to be administrators or to remain administrators. Administration is more commonly a political role, with
continuation and survival being more sought-after personal goals
than innovation and the enhancement of organizational
effectiveness.

THE MAKING OF DECISIONS

We are all accustomed in higher education to attending lots of
meetings where much is discussed but nothing gets done. Such
discussions and debates are often philosophical in nature; that is,
they focus on beliefs rather than actions. But there are actions in
higher education and they go on all the time, meetings notwith-
standing. In their most concrete form, these actions involve the
allocation of resources—positions, dollars, raises—to programs
and faculty. This is the organizational bottom line in higher education. Who gets the positions, dollars, and raises?

These decisions are made every year in every department,
school, college, and university and they are made on the same
basis. Faculty may continue to talk and debate, but through it all,
administrators divide up the money and they do so on the basis
of some criteria.

In this book we have advocated outcome management as the
basis for making resource allocation decisions, that is, giving the
resources to the programs and faculty that are productive, not to
the ones that have the most political power or to everyone equally,
regardless of performance. Dare to put your resources into productivity, and to do so publicly, and to build plans that will enable
your resources to yield even more productivity. Down the road

you can expect to have a more productive institution—and that, in the final analysis, is the true bottom line for outcome management: a more productive institution.

Bibliography

Allport, F. M. (1962). A Structuronomic Conception of Behavior: Individual and Collective. *Journal of Abnormal and Social Psychology*, 64, 3–30.

Brown, L. D. (1985). *The Quality of the Doctorate in Schools of Education.* New York: Ford Foundation.

Ferber, M. A., and Kordick, B. (1978). Sex Differentials in the Earnings of Ph.D.'s. *Industrial and Labor Relations Review*, 31, 227–238.

Festinger, L. (1954). A Theory of Social Comparison Processes. *Human Relations*, 7, 117–140.

Gagne, R. M. (1985). *The Conditions of Learning* (4th ed.). New York: Holt, Rinehart & Winston.

Glass, G. V., and Hopkins, K. D. (1984). *Statistical Methods in Education and Psychology* (2nd ed.). Englewood Cliffs, NJ: Prentice-Hall.

Heider, F. (1958). *The Psychology of Interpersonal Relations.* New York: Wiley.

Hersey, P., and Blanchard, K. H. (1977). *Management of Organizational Behavior: Utilizing Human Resources* (3rd ed.). Englewood Cliffs, NJ: Prentice-Hall.

Homans, G. (1950). *The Human Group.* New York: Harcourt Brace and World.

Hovland, C. I., Janis, I. L., and Kelley, M. M. (1953). *Communication and Persuasion.* New Haven, CT: Yale University Press.

Jewell, L. N., and Reitz, H. J. (1981). *Group Effectiveness in Organizations*. Glenview, IL: Scott, Foresman.

Kallenberg, A. L., and Sorenson, A. B. (1979). The Sociology of Labor Markets. In A. Inkeles, J. Coleman, and R.H. Turner (Eds.). *Annual Review of Sociology*. Vol. 5. Palo Alto, CA: Annual Reviews, pp. 351–379.

Katz, D. A. (1973). Faculty Salaries, Promotion, and Productivity at a Large University. *American Economic Review* 63, 469–477.

Koch, J. V., and Chizmar, J. F. (1973). The Influence of Teaching and Other Factors upon Absolute Salaries and Salary Increments at Illinois State University. *Journal of Economic Education*, 5, 27–34.

March, J. G., and Simon, H. A. (1958). *Organizations*. New York: Wiley.

Ouchi, W. G. (1981). *Theory Z: How American Business Can Meet the Japanese Challenge*. Reading, MA: Addison-Wesley.

Peters, J. T., and Waterman, R. H. (1982). *In Search of Excellence. Lessons from America's Best Run Companies*. New York: Harper & Row.

Saaty, T. L. (1977). A Scaling Method for Priorities in Hierarchical Structures. *Journal of Mathematical Psychology*, 15, 234–281.

———. (1980). *The Analytic Hierarchy Process*. New York: McGraw-Hill.

Saupe, J. L., (1978). *The Politics of Faculty Salaries*. ERIC Document Reproduction Service No. ED152 163. Los Angeles: University of Southern California.

Siegfried, J. J., and White, K. J. (1973). Financial Rewards to Research and Teaching: A Case Study of Academic Economists. *American Economic Review*, 63, 309–316.

Tolles, N. A., and Melichar, E. (1968). Studies of the Structure of Economists' Salaries and Income. *American Economic Review*, 58, 1–153.

Tuckman, H. P., and Hageman, R. P. (1976). An Analysis of the Reward Structure in Two Disciplines. *Journal of Higher Education*, 67, 447–464.

Weick, K. E. (1969). *The Social Psychology of Organizing*. Reading, MA: Addison-Wesley.

Index

About the Authors

Bruce W. Tuckman was dean of the College of Education at Florida State University for several years. He received a doctorate in psychology from Princeton University and he is a fellow of the American Psychological Association. In his capacity as dean, he undertook and carried out the activities on which *Effective College Management* is based. He is also the author of other books, including *Preparing to Teach the Disadvantaged* (with J. L. O'Brian), *Conducting Educational Research, Measuring Educational Outcomes: Fundamentals of Testing, Evaluating Instructional Programs*, and *Analyzing and and Designing Educational Research*. Presently he is professor of educational research at Florida State.

F. Craig Johnson is professor of educational research and assistant dean of education at Florida State University. He received a doctorate in communications from the University of Wisconsin. He has published numerous articles on higher education relating to the quantification of institutional research.